If you're looking for an empowering tool to help you win in leadership and in life, *The Trust Protocol* is it! This bold, thought-provoking book will bring new clarity to many of your relational, spiritual, and professional experiences and will provide the key to your success in the future. The Trust Protocol works EVERY time!

Chris Brown, nationally syndicated radio host
of *Chris Brown's True Stewardship* and host
of the *Life. Money. Hope.* podcast

Trust is the great foundation on which we build our families, workplaces, churches, friendships, and neighborhoods—that raw commitment to trust another person. It's a daring, scary reality. In *The Trust Protocol*, Mac invites us to live into this reality—not ignoring brokenness and betrayal but rather leaning into the strength of trust no matter the risk. Because the reward of deep trust is a wholly improved life.

Mark Batterson, *New York Times* bestselling author
of *The Circle Maker* and lead pastor
of National Community Church

I am excited about the journey you are about to take. The time and effort you invest in reading Mac Richard's inspired work will be repaid into the countless generations of your family who follow. Though they may never know the exact words you are about to read, the effect these words will have upon their lives in the future will cause them to remember you.

From the foreword by Andy Andrews, author of *New York Times* bestseller *The Traveler's Gift*

Anyone who has been in a leadership role (or just lived on Earth) for more than ten minutes will admit that one of the most difficult aspects of what they do is trust. As my good friend Mac Richard shares in his latest book, *The Trust Protocol*, trust is a fragile thing. But it is the most fragile things in life that are also the most valuable and worth fighting for. This book will help you fight for—and maintain—a life of trust, no matter where you live or what you do. And although it takes time and tenacity, living a life of trust is *always* worth it.

Ed Young, pastor of Fellowship Church and author
of *The Creative Leader* and *Fifty Shades of They*

Trust is a must! Mac unpacks the key essentials to building your life, and your leadership, on the basis of trust. And he challenges us all to a higher level of relationship responsibility. Practical and timely, *The Trust Protocol* will help you lead well regardless of what season you're currently in.

Brad Lomenick, former president of Catalyst and author
of *H3 Leadership* and *The Catalyst Leader*

In an age of cynicism, where people are turned off by politics and the pulpit, Mac Richard is an authentic voice of faith. I know this because he is my pastor. If I could hear one person on this planet preach about the subject of trust, it would be Mac. He gets to the heart of spiritual matters. Faith at its heart is about trust. It's one thing to believe in God; it's quite something else to trust him with our lives. We all want deeper relationships built on trust. Mac leads us down that path in this revelatory book. I commend it to you.

Rick Perry, former governor of Texas

Pastor Mac Richard has written a powerful book that is a must-read for anyone who wants and needs love. There is wisdom for everyone! People who live by the Trust Protocol understand that everything in life that really matters grows and radiates from relationships, and trust is the tie that binds any and all relationships—with God, our spouses, our friends, and our community. The more trust we have, the more influence we have, and this book teaches us a process for building the single greatest human trait we can possibly develop—being trustworthy.

Buzz Williams, head coach, Virginia Tech men's basketball

The kind of wisdom contained in *The Trust Protocol* doesn't come the easy way. In his new book, Mac shares from his valuable life experience how to not only earn trust but also keep it.

Steven Furtick, pastor of Elevation Church
and *New York Times* bestselling author

Nobody lives and teaches leadership like Mac Richard. He is a leader of leaders with proven experience learned in the trenches. *The Trust Protocol* gives both brilliant insights and practical strategies to raise your leadership to the next level. Do yourself a favor and get this book and everything Mac puts out on leadership!

Jud Wilhite, senior pastor of Central Church
and author of *Pursued*

In everything I've had the opportunity to be a part of—my faith, marriage, parenting, and Crossfit—success or failure really comes down to the choices we make and the people around us. In *The Trust Protocol*, Mac explains clearly how powerful we really are when we align our walk and our talk and how to use that power to make the world a better place.

Rich Froning Jr., four-time individual and two-time
Affiliate Cup CrossFit Games champion

Here's what you need to know about *The Trust Protocol*: relationships are important; good relationships are built on trust; trust shows the reliability and strength of an individual. Mac does a phenomenal job detailing why trust is so important and how to implement his Trust Protocol into your life. Do yourself a favor and check this book out.

Levi Lusko, author of *Swipe Right: The Life-and-Death
Power of Sex and Romance*

THE TRUST PROTOCOL

The Key to Building
Stronger Families, Teams,
and Businesses

MAC RICHARD

BakerBooks

a division of Baker Publishing Group
www.BakerBooks.com

Published by Baker Books
a division of Baker Publishing Group
PO Box 6287, Grand Rapids, MI 49516-6287
www.bakerbooks.com

Printed in the United States of America

Library of Congress Cataloging-in-Publication Data
Names: Richard, Mac, 1966– author.
Title: The trust protocol : the key to building stronger families, teams, and
    businesses / Mac Richard.
Description: Grand Rapids : Baker Books, 2017. | Includes bibliographical
    references.
Identifiers: LCCN 2017026982 | ISBN 9780801019647 (pbk.)
Subjects: LCSH: Trust—Religious aspects—Christianity. | Interpersonal
    relations—Religious aspects—Christianity. | Responsibility—Religious
    aspects—Christianity.
Classification: LCC BV4597.53.T78 R53 2017 | DDC 248.4—dc23
LC record available at https://lccn.loc.gov/2017026982

The Proprietor is represented by The FEDD Agency, Inc.

17 18 19 20 21 22 23   7 6 5 4 3 2 1

For Julie

Contents

Foreword

Have you ever met someone with whom you shared an instant connection? Yep. Me too.

Have you ever met someone with whom you instantly connected and, in the days and weeks that followed, kept in touch with that person and became real, actual friends? Good. Again, me too.

Okay . . . how about this: Have you ever met someone, instantly connected, and in the days and weeks that followed, talked on the phone twice and had lunch together once before booking airline tickets for your family to go out of the country with that person and their spouse? And stay in the same house together? For a week?

You're a "no" on that one? Well, I'm a "yes." Because that is exactly what happened when I met Mac Richard.

In truth, I don't really remember the moment we met. I've known the man for only ten years or so, but I *feel* like we've been buddies for much longer. It's an odd thing, I know, but sometimes I have to make myself remember that I did not grow up with Mac. I didn't meet him until I was in my forties.

The same goes for Mac's wife, Julie, even though my wife, Polly, and I tell folks that we have known Julie for years. Of course, I'm sure we are no different from anyone else fortunate enough to spend an hour with Julie. She makes it easy to feel as though you have known her for years.

Curiously, I believe that how they are—the way Mac and Julie live their lives—makes it very easy to bond quickly with them. There is a spark in their spirit, an openness about them, a magnetic joy that makes one feel as though . . . well, like you've known them your entire life.

Actually, I suppose you'd *have* to feel like you knew someone a long time to go away together for a week . . . staying in the same place . . . no locked doors between you at night . . . with your children there as well . . . sheesh!

To even attempt this scenario would require a whole lot of trust on the part of someone. In fact, a lot of trust would be required of *every*one.

Doesn't it take time to trust someone? you ask. That is what we seem to believe, and partly because of that I'll respond with "Usually, yes." Most of us consider trust to be built slowly, with verification, and in degrees. Like the finest Middle Eastern balsamic or the most expensive German Riesling, trust is created by a combination of things and, while the end result is almost magical, the process cannot be rushed.

So, if trust cannot be rushed, how in the world was it possible for Polly to have been thrilled to have a couple—a couple she had only met one time—join our family *on the only vacation* we would ever take celebrating our twenty-fifth wedding anniversary? At the end of the day, I suppose, one could say that it was because my wife trusts *me*. She trusts my discernment and my judgment. But wait . . . she trusted *my* judgment? That's nice, but all I did was trust Mac.

Here, I believe, is the best question you could ask about that situation: Andy, why did you trust Mac right away?

Why? First, know this: should you decide to search and find the answer to that question, and should you choose to incorporate its principles into your everyday thought process—the answer will, quite literally, change your life and legacy.

At this present time, there are certain relationship realities, personal outcomes, and professional results in your life that, for the most part, you have considered adequate. That is all about to change. The answer to the question above possesses the power to initiate a seismic shift in your thinking. At the moment you find it, there will be *recognition*.

This crucial step of identifying the answer will lead you to *comprehension*. Be warned, however. Comprehension is not your desired destination.

Comprehension is merely a foyer leading into the beautiful areas you will experience by entering the whole house of understanding. For when you possess a *deep understanding* of the principles contained in the answer, you will have a vastly different vision of the life God has planned for you and your family.

Hmm . . . you wonder . . . really? God has a life planned for my family and me?

Yes, he does, but hang on a minute. At this point, it would be irresponsible for me not to remind you that God had a promised land planned for the children of Israel too.

Unfortunately, because of a few things some of them did (that they should not have done) and a few other things some did not do (that they *should* have done), there were actually children of Israel who lived out their days on earth without ever entering the promised land. In other words, they died never having lived the amazing life God had planned for them.

Fortunately, the answer you seek—along with answers to questions you've not yet asked—is explained throughout the pages of the book you hold in your hands.

I am excited about the journey you are about to take. The time and effort you invest in reading Mac Richard's inspired work will be repaid into the countless generations of your family who follow. Though they may never know the exact words you are about to read, the effect these words will have upon their lives in the future will cause them to remember you.

Decades from now, stories will be told, and perhaps there will be a portrait of you somewhere in their homes. Family legends will emerge, as they always do, and from time to time, someone will direct a guest's attention to the portrait. "That's the one I was telling you about," they'll say. "That's who pointed our family in a direction. That is who made certain that we all understood the Trust Protocol."

Andy Andrews

Acknowledgments

I t's more than a little overwhelming to realize how many people helped, coached, prodded, critiqued, encouraged, and challenged me to finally bring this book into the world. It's even more overwhelming to realize I can never repay them, but my gratitude is deep and real.

To Chad Allen and his amazing team at Baker Books, thank you for taking a shot on a first-time author and believing not only in this book and what it can be but also in me personally. Your hand and patience in helping me navigate the publishing waters for the first time were invaluable.

To Jack Kuhatschek, your editing expertise was only surpassed by your grace and humor. I actually looked forward to receiving your notes and critiques, not only because they were sorely needed but also because they were always delivered with humor and encouragement.

To Esther Fedorkevich, I'm incredibly grateful for your pull-no-punches, cut-to-the-chase style and the drive you brought to making this a reality. Thanks too to everyone at the Fedd Group and for your excitement, proficiency, and skill. I had a ball getting to do this with you.

Andy Andrews, I could never ever, ever, ever have known how faxing something from the Orange Beach, Alabama, Pack & Mail would turn into one of the great blessings and friendships of my and my family's lives. Your constant encouragement, hard-won wisdom, and deep well of experience were fuel to my fire. You and Polly, Austin and Adam mean the world to us.

Web Smith, you not only trained me and honed my cat-like quickness, you also pushed me to write and tell stories that help people.

Pastors David and Lisa Hughes, your no-matter-what friendship through thick and thin came into our lives when Julie and I needed it most. As David says, "The only thing wrong with our friendship is that we haven't known each other for forty years."

Ben Young, your friendship and mentorship since I was in sixth grade all the way to this day and this book are absolutely priceless. Through every season of life, you've been a friend I could trust, learn from, and laugh with. I'll take a Diablo sandwich and a Dr Pepper . . . YOU WANT SOMETHIN'??

Dr. and Mrs. Ed Young, through Second Baptist Church in Houston, you showed me what it means to *be* the church when the world crumbled under our family's feet in seventh grade. You taught me and showed me what it means to have a relationship with Christ, you were the vehicle through whom God called me to pastoral ministry, and you're the reason I met Julie Sanderson. Your commitment to God, each other, your family, Scripture, and evangelism are examples we draw from every day and will for the rest of our lives.

Pastors Ed and Lisa Young, you took me—literally, right out of college—into your home and your lives and showed Julie and me what it looks like to love and lead at home and in the church. Ed, you got me hooked on tarpon fishing and fishing for men. Your friendship and the years we've shared are our greatest blessing outside of our immediate family. You're my pastor, Pastor!

To the Lake Hills Church family, for someone who speaks for a living, it's so difficult to put into words how grateful we are for you. For your love, your faithfulness, the witness and safe place you provided Emily and Joseph as they grew up, and so much more, thank you. We love you and can't wait to see what God has prepared for us to do together over the next twenty years and beyond!

Gill and Patrick, your friendship, love, and laughter have been the greatest blessing a brother could ask for. I'm proud to be your brother.

Mom, you taught me the love and power of words. You are the greatest teacher I've ever had or known. But more than anything, you taught three boys unconditional love. You stayed. You stayed, you prayed, you worked, and you fought, and you showed us how to love, no matter what. We never would've made it without you. To raise three sons by yourself who all turned out to be more or less contributing members of society, married to godly wives, and enjoying the blessings of family you missed is a legacy we can only hope to emulate. I love you.

Emily and Joseph, thank you for being more than your mom and I knew enough to pray for. Watching you step more and more fully into who God created you to be is the greatest reward and biggest payoff we've ever known.

And, above all, to Julie—I love you with everything I have. The first twenty-six years have been so far above and beyond anything I could imagine or ask for. Your faith, joy, beauty, intelligence, work ethic, sense of humor, loyalty, and wisdom—the Proverbs 31 woman can't even see your taillights. You're just the best.

Introduction

About the time Julie and I moved to Austin, we discovered that a very close friend of ours was a habitual liar. I don't mean that he was an acquaintance or someone we knew in passing. I mean our families prayed together, did life together, and were fully invested in each other's lives.

A mutual friend had uncovered his trail of deceit and then called us to describe the long and winding road of lies and fabrications he had paved. The scope of this dishonesty ran from the mundane to the majestic. Everything from his résumé to his daily routine was a patchwork of minor falsehoods and outright fraud.

And we never saw it coming.

His integrity was considered absolutely above reproach. We all thought he was a godly, diligent, and successful over-achiever who was setting an ethical pace for the rest of us to follow.

We were both rocked to the core. Because the allegations were so disorienting, my first thought was, *There's no way this is true . . . someone's setting him up. Maybe even the friend who told us.*

My mind was racing trying to discern who was really telling the truth: Was it the friend who claimed this guy was a habitual liar? Was the alleged habitual liar being set up for some nefarious reason that I couldn't imagine? For forty-five minutes, of all the people in my day-to-day world, Julie was the only person I *knew* I could trust. It felt like the earth was shifting under my feet, and I couldn't find anywhere stable to stand.

This book is about what took place on the other side of those forty-five minutes.

Since 2000, the Edelman Trust Barometer has surveyed thousands of people around the world gauging their confidence in government, businesses, media, and nongovernment organizations (NGOs). For the first time ever, the 2017 Edelman Trust Barometer found that trust in all four categories fell from the previous year. Fewer than half of those surveyed expressed even an average level of trust in those institutions.[1]

The political rise of both Bernie Sanders and Donald Trump in the 2016 presidential campaign revealed a visceral disconnect created almost exclusively by politicians repeatedly breaking trust with the electorate. Too many athletes to count who were once celebrated for their exploits on the field have been humiliated by revelations of their deliberate cheating and have damaged the integrity of the games they play. A fraction of the clergy has not only forfeited its authority to lead spiritually by preying on children, but a significant contingent also conspired to hide and often perpetuate colleagues' predatory behavior across generations.

These cultural and institutional examples, as toxic and demoralizing as they are, actually reflect what we know to be true personally: trust is a fragile thing.

And this is our great opportunity.

When we commit ourselves to being people of trust, we build, strengthen, and fortify the very thing that holds homes, neighborhoods, businesses, and teams together. When we hold each other accountable and allow ourselves to be held accountable, we begin to solidify the relational ground under our feet. And when the relational ground is stable, everything is stronger, healthier, and better. All of a sudden, the trust generated between a husband and wife or a parent and child begins to spill over into our neighborhoods and schools. People who cultivate trust in their personal lives and most intimate relationships attract like-minded people. When they go into business together or partner together on projects and deals, they develop and distribute more of that trust, and everyone benefits.

As I processed through the doubt and uncertainty prompted by our friend's deceit, I began to pray through not only my emotions—which were redlining at the moment—but also through the facts that I knew. The inconsistencies and patterns of deceit were undeniable, but I still wondered, *Could they have been orchestrated by our friend who discovered them?*

Then I realized something: for him to have orchestrated and substantiated those accusations would have required an elaborate conspiracy with multiple other people being in on it. And they were all people whom we had known for years. It was the fact of the collective trust all those other people had amassed over the years that revealed beyond a reasonable

21

doubt who was trustworthy and who was not. In the ensuing weeks and months, all the facts exposed the truth that had been only partially revealed initially.

John Adams said, "Facts are stubborn things; and whatever may be our wishes, our inclinations, or the dictates of our passion, they cannot alter the state of facts and evidence."[2]

Our faith is proved by our actions: *faith without works is dead*. Faith *with* works is alive and vital, powerful and effective, beautiful and strong. Faith with works improves and enriches every relationship, team, church, business, neighborhood, and school it impacts.

Welcome to the Trust Protocol.

1

"I Love You, and I Will Fire You"

Introducing the Trust Protocol

Straight out of college, I got the kind of opportunity that most graduates only dream of. I was the third person hired by a start-up that erupted in exponential growth. The job found me before I graduated because of a friendship with the guy who would become the leader of this start-up. We were all overworked and underpaid, and we wouldn't have traded it for anything else in the world. I loved what I was doing, the adventure of doing something new and unknown, and the people. In the words of one early associate, it was a "rocket ship."

One day Ed called me into his office. I came in, and he asked me to close the door behind me. I sat down for what I thought would be one of our usual conversations: how things were going in my department, what was up with my girlfriend, or some new initiative/event/strategy that he had cooked up. At the time, Ed was only twenty-nine years old, but even then he had a natural leadership presence, the ability to cut through clutter, a monster work ethic, and a passion that was infectious. The conversation went like this:

> Ed: Mac, sit down. I want to talk to you. You know I love that you're here.
>
> Mac: Thanks, I appreciate it. I love being here, and I'm having a ball.
>
> Ed: Man, I'm glad. I really believe in you and think you've got amazing potential. And you know I think you're a great guy. [Did I mention he was very perceptive? I was so green I never saw the big hairy "but" that was obviously lurking in this opening statement.] But you need to understand something: I love you, and I will fire you.
>
> Mac: [internally] *Well, then could you maybe love me just a little less?*
>
> Ed: I can't keep paying you just because you're a good guy. You've got too much talent, and we've got too much to do for me to let you get by without producing something and being a contributor around here. You've got great potential, but from now on, *potential* is profanity for you. All it means is that you haven't done anything yet.

I won't bore you with the rest of the conversation, except to say that he did not fire me, though he would've been more than justified on more than a few occasions. And almost twenty years later, we remain very close. Our friendship has not only survived, it has also thrived, not in spite of that conversation and others like it but largely because of them.

Would it surprise you to know that the start-up was actually a church? Or that Ed was the pastor of that church? I mean, what *pastor* says, "I love you, and I will fire you"? The pastor was—and is—Ed Young, and the church is Fellowship Church, which began in Dallas–Ft. Worth and now has locations across the country and is one of the most innovative, influential churches of this generation.

I would love to tell you that in that moment I realized God was using Ed to shape me and mold me, so I joyfully submitted. The reality, though, is that I did exactly what most of us do when we feel threatened or vulnerable: I read the situation through the lens of self—specifically, self-protection and self-preservation. I feared for my job, worried about where I would go should I actually get fired, and was unsure how I would explain losing my first job right out of college.

But in God's truly amazing grace, another lesson revealed itself through that same lens of self. I realized that staying in that situation, working for Ed, and submitting to his leadership, in addition to being the right thing to do was actually in my best interest. Where else would someone have more of my best interest at heart? Where else would I never have conflict or disagreement? Where else could I find someone with whom I always agreed? I realized that I would get better, I would be better, if I let him hold me accountable and push me.

What I couldn't know at the time was that that defining moment early in my ministry was carving in stone for me the absolute, undeniable power of the Trust Protocol.

The Trust Protocol

In Hebrews 10:24, the Bible challenges Christ followers: "And let us consider how we may spur one another on toward love and good deeds." In that simple, one-sentence exhortation, God asserts and reinforces the Trust Protocol, which is essential and fundamental to all he has called us to be and do in relationship with him. Not only is it woven into every page and principle of Scripture, it is also absolutely essential to everything that really matters to us—our families and relationships, our vocation and work, our purpose and fulfillment. The power of this Protocol can actually help us point people toward a relationship with Christ *before* they ever discover that the Bible is reliable.

There are a few things you need to know before we dive into the Trust Protocol:

1. The Trust Protocol works. Every single time. We'll talk about why this is true in detail in the last chapter. But for now, just know that whenever we choose to put it into effect, regardless of the context or circumstances, it produces results so powerful, so beautiful that nothing else compares to it. No exceptions.

2. The Trust Protocol is hard work. There's just no way around it. This is not a game for the faint of heart or the timid. For this to work, we have to roll up our sleeves and put our spiritual, emotional, and relational—and sometimes, even our physical—weight into it.

3. The Trust Protocol will get messy. By virtue of the fact that it calls for fallen and fallible people to truly engage with one another, just know that it will get messy at some points along the way.

And perhaps most important,

4. The work, the mess, the pain and uncertainty along the way—all of it—is absolutely worth it. If you're currently participating in the Trust Protocol (though you may never have used that terminology), you're going to be affirmed and encouraged throughout this book. If you've not used it intentionally or consistently, you're going to discover the supernatural blessing that God pours out on every relationship, enterprise, and exercise that practices the Protocol.

I want to set your expectations before we actually begin so that, should you choose to participate in the Protocol, you do so with your eyes wide open and are as prepared as you can be for what follows.

What exactly is the Trust Protocol? It is simply this: *forging credibility through integrity and action*. It is deliberately demonstrating our dependability to the people with whom we live, work, love, and serve—when we excel and, especially, when we struggle. It is backing up our talk with our walk. It is being consistently the same person we were created to be no matter where we are or whom we are with.

The Trust Protocol calls us to a higher plane of relational responsibility. Instead of assigning blame and fault to others for disasters and disappointments, practitioners of the Protocol assume *accurate and appropriate* ownership for their role in those failures and learn from their mistakes. Instead of blithely getting through another day of the status quo, the Trust Protocol propels us through intentional interactions that invigorate community, connectedness, and collaboration. This relational responsibility feeds the fire of trust and smokes out those unwilling to pay the price to stoke that fire.

Everything in life that really matters radiates out of relationships. From the lunchroom to the locker room, from the bedroom to the boardroom, regardless of the arena or the endeavor, relationship is the coin of the realm. And trust, or credibility, is the tie that binds every relationship, from the most casual acquaintance, to the marketplace, to the most intimate and personal connections of marriage and family.

The Universal Value of Trust

By any objective standard, my wife, Julie, and I live in the greatest city in the world. Austin, Texas, is home to the weird, the wonderful, and the wacky of every imaginable stripe. Every year, Austin welcomes tens of thousands of new residents from around the world chasing the dream of launching technology start-ups. Many of these new arrivals can describe in vivid detail what their businesses will do and who their target market might be, and their businesses are as varied and diverse as the imaginations that dream them up. But whenever I ask about their challenges, what might be their obstacles to growth or corporate survival, without exception they point to interpersonal issues as the primary impediment to organizational success.

Interestingly, but not surprisingly, those are the same challenges and issues that churches struggle with. The preaching, connecting and assimilating, discipling, mission strategizing—these are easy in comparison with the people issues that we encounter on a regular basis. I've noticed a common thread that runs through every single industry, enterprise, and vocation: people. No matter what we do or where we do it, we're all in the people business, and how we navigate the relational waters of our everyday lives is the single greatest propellant or deterrent to how successful, how fulfilled, how peaceful, and how effective we will be.

Relationships come in all shapes and sizes, with wildly varying needs, expectations, and requirements. But deliberately and intentionally forging credibility that anchors the Trust Protocol boils down to a single, simple element: integrity. Every relationship, no matter how superficial and temporary, or long-term and intimate, can be rock solid *if* it is built on a foundation of integrity.

Relationships are unavoidable. Relationships of integrity are invincible. Integrity, which we'll cover later in more detail, means so much more than mere honesty or ethical behavior. Those things do matter, and they're mandatory for our relational and professional success over time. But if we limit the meaning to merely telling the truth and honoring our contracts—legal or relational—then we've set the bar far too low for what God declares our integrity standard to be.

Foundations of the Trust Protocol

When I was in the sixth grade, Dr. Edwin Young (Ed's dad) had become the pastor of my home church, Second Baptist Church, in Houston. Almost immediately, Dr. Young cranked up our church's engine, excitement, and impact. At the time, Ed was a senior in high school who was about to depart for Florida State University where he would play basketball on scholarship.

Over the next few years, Ed would be the counselor we would fight to have on Beach Retreat, our annual summer camp. He would sneak us out in the middle of the night to go get breakfast at Mr. Z's, South Padre Island's finest all-night diner. We fished in the resort's pond. From our condo's balcony! Since it was the early '80s, Ed lathered up in sunscreen, tied a black headband around his head, and brandishing an M-16 water gun stormed the beach for freedom, justice, and the American way, a la Rambo.

The summer before my senior season of high school basketball, Ed stopped me and told me he was going to start training me in the church's weight room. Every day, we'd meet in that shed, and he'd put me through reps and sets he'd learned at Florida State. On the opening night of the season, my Lee Generals squared off against Ed's alma mater Memorial High School, and there was Ed in the stands, watching and cheering me on.

We reconnected when Ed returned to finish college in Houston after marrying Lisa and joined the staff at Second Baptist. I'd regularly stop by his converted office above the sanctuary, attend retreats that he planned as our college minister, and would house-sit for him and Lisa when they went on vacation.

By the time Ed looked across his desk and said, "I love you, and I will fire you," we had accumulated more than ten years of shared history, relationship, and life. I knew that he did in fact love me. And I sensed a very real sincerity that he would in fact fire me. In short, I trusted him.

The Trust Protocol is an absolute nonnegotiable in every enterprise and exercise that matters. Partnerships that practice the Protocol persist. They survive economic downturns and pricing wars, damaging words, thoughtlessness, out-of-the-ordinary unkindnesses, and frequently even out-and-out betrayals. The beautiful power of the Trust Protocol lies in the fact that it is available to anyone and everyone who wants to make a difference in this world:

- The fourth-grade teacher who has influenced and inspired generations of students to enjoy learning and seek out new subjects to study
- The husband and wife who not only stay together for a lifetime but who actually enjoy each other as much in their seventies as they did on their honeymoon
- The entrepreneurial business owner whose employees know that their boss takes home less money personally so they can participate in the company's profit-sharing program
- The church that evolves across decades and remains a lighthouse and beacon of hope as their neighborhood shifts demographically

These and so many others are practitioners of the Protocol.

A *protocol* is simply a predetermined procedure or set of rules. It establishes a process or system, whether in diplomatic circles or scientific and medical experiments. Protocols also play a role in spycraft. Think Jack Bauer and Chloe O'Brian in *24* or Carrie Mathis and Saul Berenson in *Homeland*. When Saul walks past an operative in a crowded European town square, the red carnation in his lapel indicates that their mission is a "go." Protocols provide next steps in if-then sequences: if *this* happens, then *that* should follow.

31

The Trust Protocol is an if-then sequence: if love, then good deeds. Everywhere the Trust Protocol is practiced, love and good deeds are always at work. Here's why: love without action is bankrupt, and action without love is hollow. But together, love and good deeds conspire to cultivate trust and unity that change everything they touch for the better.

This was the exact tension Ed was living in and living out that day he called me into his office. There was genuine love and concern for me as a person, friend, and leader-in-training. But his investment in me as a person didn't eclipse his larger responsibility to the church as a whole.

It was his responsibility for both me personally and the church at large that compelled him to hold my feet to the fire—to hold me accountable for my actions (or lack thereof). He made the time to spur me to good deeds precisely *because* he loved me and cared about growth and development and productivity—both mine and the church's. It wasn't that he would fire me *despite* his love for me. Rather, he was willing to go through the relational discomfort *because* he loved me. He wouldn't allow me to settle for some warm and fuzzy, saccharine substitute for love. He forced me to realize that if my love for people in the church and outside the church was real, then I would back it up with real action, with productivity and effectiveness. In short, with good deeds.

I'm now more than twenty years removed from that conversation, but I'm even more amazed at the extravagant goodness of God, who allows us, even *calls* us, to participate with him in the divinely ordained Trust Protocol. In those twenty intervening years, I have seen the Protocol repeatedly reap staggering results in countless homes, teams, churches, and businesses. Anywhere and everywhere that it is adopted and embraced and practiced—parenting, ministry, the marketplace, nonprofits, even in government, politics, and athletics—everything works better.

Let us consider how we may spur one another on toward love and good deeds. It's so simple, isn't it? But don't let simple lull you into thinking it's easy. In fact, it may be the most difficult thing in the world to do. To live out the Trust Protocol is to guarantee difficulty, hurt, heartache, disappointment, misunderstanding, restlessness, doubt, uncertainty, trauma, drama, and anger. And, *spoiler alert*: it's most difficult where it's most crucial—with the people closest to you.

But those who do practice the Protocol get to partake in the transcendent blessing and gift of genuine connectedness, eternity-shaking effectiveness, changed lives, genuine intimacy, abundant life, and the thrill of adventure.

The flip side of that coin is also true: wherever the Trust Protocol is missing, neglected, or omitted, we find brokenness, fear, resentment, callousness, isolation, and cynicism. Veteran political consultant Steve Schmidt, in the months leading up to the 2016 election, observed, "Trust has completely collapsed between every single institution—with the exception of the US military—and the American people. This has led to distrust of politicians and a belief by many that the country is headed in the wrong direction. . . . When trust collapses and institutions fail, all of the old rules are out the window."[1]

Our world is literally dying for the Trust Protocol to work, which means it's time for us to get to work.

2

The Battle of the *Why*

Establishing and Evaluating Motive

In the early years of Twitter, I remember following a Twitter fight between a very prominent pastor with a worldwide ministry and someone I'd never heard of. (By the way, say *Twitter fight* out loud. Go ahead, I'll wait. Can we not all agree that a Twitter fight is every bit as silly as it sounds? Ain't *nobody* got time for that.) As I looked on this brewing argument, in 140 characters or less, they began going back and forth at each other with rapid-fire returns. It was like watching Forrest Gump winning the gold medal in Ping-Pong.

After a few flurries and salvoes, I got curious about the prominent pastor's opponent. I clicked on his profile and discovered that the world-famous pastor was down in the mud with a guy who had all of forty-seven followers. Now, to be abundantly clear, in God's economy that lesser-known pastor has every bit as much value and significance as the prominent pastor. Obviously. But I couldn't help but think, *How much oxygen did that well-known pastor with worldwide influence and inspiration just burn up with an argument that never should've seen the light of day? How much of his clearly limited time and energy and passion did he just spend on something that almost none of his family, staff, church, friends, or followers would have seen except that he chose to bring it to the stage?*

Once you begin deliberately practicing the Trust Protocol, you're going to notice that the more trust you build, the more influence you have. When people learn they can trust you, they will seek you out as a source of help, wisdom, and encouragement that will add value to their lives or projects. It is at exactly this point that everything—I mean *everything*—is in jeopardy and up for grabs.

Some of the most profound spiritual challenges we ever face are our failures in handling temptations, struggles, and difficulties. God frequently uses these challenges to lead us back to where our hearts and minds should always be: on our knees, worshiping, pursuing, and loving him. Counterintuitively, then, success and winning set the stage for an even more difficult, and more revealing, battle, for it's in victory, success, and prosperity that our spiritual health and vitality are truly seen. When we win, do we worship God or congratulate ourselves?

When our influence, input, or work is in demand, the greatest battles will be waged. They occur in secret, subterranean chambers of our hearts because it's there that we decide why we're doing what we're doing. *What* we're doing may not change superficially; we may still do the exact same things, talk about the same subjects, promote the same efforts, and publicize the same business in the same ways. Deciding *why* we're doing those things will make all the difference in the world. At this point, we have to choose: self or others? Am I doing this to build my ego, my wealth, or my status? Or am I doing this to serve, equip, empower, and encourage others to be and do what God has created them to be and do?

One of the things I love about the Bible is that the lead characters are frequently flawed. Significantly flawed. Consider for a moment an argument that broke out among the disciples—at the Last Supper, no less—over who would be the greatest among them.

> Then they began to argue among themselves about who would be the greatest among them. Jesus told them, "In this world the kings and great men lord it over their people, yet they are called 'friends of the people.' But among you it will be different. Those who are the greatest among you should take the lowest rank, and the leader should be like a servant. Who is more important, the one who sits at the table or the one who serves? The one who sits at the table, of course. But not here! For I am among you as one who serves." (Luke 22:24–27 NLT)

Here is the handpicked small group of men who would be charged with the responsibility of launching a worldwide ministry after Jesus's ascension, and they are openly quarreling about who'll get the corner office.

This is the battle of the *why*. The disciples departed from the upper room that night, witnessed the crucifixion, the resurrection, and the ensuing forty days of Jesus's life on earth, and then lived out the rest of their lives and died as martyrs. If they had done all that for their own self-aggrandizement and to raise their stock in people's eyes or even their own estimation, they would have lost the battle of the *why*. But, if they proceeded to live out their lives and die for their faith in Christ to see him glorified and his church multiplied, then victory in the battle of the *why* would be theirs.

The margin of victory in the battle of the *why* is razor thin. The margin is motive. Why are you building trust, why are you promoting your cause, your services, your business, your ideas, your books, your Instagram account or Facebook page? Why?

I would love to tell you that I don't understand how the disciples could have ever wondered about who would be the greatest. I would love to say that status, or the size of Lake Hills Church relative to other churches, or books sold, or any number of other metrics, never cross my mind. Unfortunately, though, the simple fact is that I'm vulnerable to all of that and more. I think, however, that realization and acknowledgment of that vulnerability goes a long way toward shoring up our defenses. When we acknowledge a weakness or a blind spot, we can then take measures to defend against it.

Every car has blind spots, areas that are hidden from view by the frame of the car. They're typically on the side and in the rear. It's not necessarily a design flaw; it's just the reality that the same frame that protects passengers also obstructs vision.

Most of our personal blind spots are on the side and to the rear. They're the peripheral and rearview issues that we often don't realize are affecting our motives, our personal battle of the *why*. A peripheral issue may be the pressure we feel to provide for our families, which drives us to work and earn a living. But a blind spot might be that we then start to work chronically so as to create a lifestyle that earns people's admiration at the expense of time with the very family for whom we started out wanting to provide.

A rearview blind spot could be the approval of a parent that was always just out of reach for us as children, but because that longing continues to drive us to strive and achieve, we push our own kids—to their detriment and our own. It may be more severe than the longing for parental approval. When people are abused and neglected, what was suffered in childhood can sometimes erroneously convince them that they're not worthy of love or respect, and they settle for whatever affection or tolerance they can get.

Fortunately, blind spots can be fixed. The remedy for those blind spots is mirrors. Mirrors in vehicles allow us to see things we can't see from our vantage point in the driver's seat. In yet another expression of God's amazing grace, he provides a variety of mirrors that reveal and remove our blind spots. I don't know that you can rank the following in priority, because God uses them collaboratively, but one does carry with it an authority that supersedes the other two.

Scripture is the primary mirror God provides us to measure our motives. It is authoritative because it is directly from God: "All Scripture is God-breathed and is useful for teaching, rebuking, correcting and training in righteousness, so that the servant of God may be thoroughly equipped for every good work" (2 Tim. 3:16–17).

Jesus affirmed the authority of Scripture when he declared that every jot and tittle of Scripture will be fulfilled (Matt.

5:18). We would say that every *i* will be dotted and every *t* will be crossed. The fact remains that *all* of the Bible is from God. It is, therefore, the authority on what is real and true, so it is the standard against which every thought, every motive, every action, and every word is evaluated.

There are a lot of books we can read, but they don't have the same impact or penetrate our lives in the same way as the Word of God. It's not simply that we read the Bible. The issue is that unlike any other book, when we read the Bible, the Bible reads us. It gives us the clearest, truest picture of who we are and what we do. I think this is why so many people work so hard to discount and denigrate the Bible; if I can diminish its authority, then that gives me license to do whatever I want to do when I want to do it and to provide whatever justification I can dream up. But if the Bible really is God's Word as it claims to be, then I ought to either conform to its standards or openly admit that I just don't care what it says and will do whatever I please.

King David wrote, "Search me, God, and know my heart . . . see if there is any offensive way in me" (Ps. 139:23–24). Because the Bible is God-breathed, the Holy Spirit reads right along with us and prompts us, challenges us, and rebukes and corrects us in order to conform us more completely to Christ's image. Sometimes, this is a painful process. Sometimes, it requires repentance, a changed mind and a changed heart that are sensitive and responsive to God's leading.

The second mirror God gives us to eliminate blind spots is prayer. Prayer is that two-way communication between God and us that engages us deeply and relationally with the One who created us for relationship. Of course, some people consider prayer one-way communication that is, in fact, very superficial, but that's not what God designed or desires it to be.

> The weapons we fight with are not the weapons of the world. On the contrary, they have divine power to demolish strongholds. We demolish arguments and every pretension that sets itself up against the knowledge of God, and we take captive every thought to make it obedient to Christ. (2 Cor. 10:4–5)

The third mirror God provides for our benefit is godly counsel. In his amazing grace and perfect wisdom, God meets our desperate need for accountability and counsel within the context of community and connectedness with other people. After twenty years of pastoring the amazing people who make up Lake Hills Church, I've noticed a pattern. At first, it gave rise to a theory, but I've seen it played out so many times and with such relentless consistency that I think it may be a spiritual law. Consider the following hypothetical illustration.

A person—we'll call him Alan—gets married, and he and his wife have a couple of kids. Early on, they're a part of a church—involved, inviting, investing, and doing all the things committed Christ followers do. Over time, though, the kids' extracurricular schedules intensify, Alan's career starts to gain momentum, and their engagement level in the church takes a slight hit. The kids hit middle school and high school and Alan's career is just kicking into overdrive, which is especially timely because he's got college to pay for soon and a wedding at some point in the not-too-distant future. Again, the time and the energy for church and the people they used to do life with just aren't there, so the people in his life who know him, whom he trusts enough to be honest, open, and vulnerable with, just aren't there. He's got friends at work and other dads he knows from his kids' activities, but they don't *really* know each other.

Where Alan goes from this point is anyone's guess. He may or may not develop a habit, relationship, or addiction that distracts him from God's will and principles. He may or may not invest more in his career than in his marriage and family. What *is* certain is that he is not growing in his faith the way he once did, and there's absolutely no way that happens without consequences of some kind.

That's the pattern. Here's the principle: No one moves away from godly community and healthy connectedness and becomes more like Jesus. God in his creative genius meets each of us personally and individually right where we are and immediately invites us into the family of faith. There he begins working on us, growing, encouraging, challenging, and equipping us for good works that he's already planned out for us in Christ Jesus (Eph. 2:10).

Spiritual growth, Christlikeness, always happens in the context of community. While faith in Christ is personal, it is never individual or isolated. We need people around us who will tell us what we need to hear and not just what we want to hear. That's the foundational, spiritual, God-given truth and mystery of the Trust Protocol. Proverbs 27 says,

> Better is open rebuke
>   than hidden love.
> Wounds from a friend can be trusted,
>   but an enemy multiplies kisses. (vv. 5–6)

Wounds from a friend . . . Only a true friend confronts us, challenges us, and rebukes us. If we're not willing to do that, then we're only an acquaintance or a colleague. True friends hold up the mirror of Scripture for us to see where we're off base and offer godly counsel on how to get back on track.

Such a friend must also be someone who loves the Lord more than they love themselves or us, someone who realizes and values the authority of Scripture and has it hidden in their heart. And it must be someone who not only loves us but also likes us. They have to like us and want only God's best for us in order for us to trust them. Without that affinity, that kinship and friendship factor, we won't fully trust them with our hearts, our motives, or our *whys*. And unless we trust them with everything, there will be parts of our lives hidden from the light of godly counsel and biblical truth.

A few years ago, we invited our good friend Andy Andrews to speak at a Fearless Family event we hosted at Lake Hills Church. Andy is a world-renowned speaker and bestselling author, with an incredible "get-it" factor. He is, like the title character in one of his bestselling books, a *noticer*. But we invited him to speak to families because we've gotten to be good friends with him and his family, and we know that he and his wife, Polly, are raising two incredible young men in their sons, Austin and Adam.

At one point in the evening, Andy told the story of how as a matter of parenting, he encourages his boys to speak to and engage with the trash collectors who pick up their garbage each week and to tell them thank you whenever they see them. He then mentioned that his trash cans are always set back straight and neat after they're emptied, though he's noticed that most of his neighbors' trash cans just get thrown down in the general vicinity of where they were picked up.

When we opened the floor for a Q&A session, one of the first question cards read, "Shouldn't we teach our children to be polite and grateful to the trash collectors just because it's the right thing to do and not so they'll set the cans back straight?"

Of course we do the right thing because it's the right thing and not so that we'll get special favors! If you do the right thing to get special favors, then it's not the right thing anymore; you've lost the battle of the *why*. Our motives have been corrupted, and our self-interest has tainted and stained the *right thing* we were attempting. Over time, self-interest will ultimately reveal itself.

I told you at the beginning of this chapter that your influence will expand as you participate in the Trust Protocol and people discover your trustability. And that is absolutely true. But there's something about the battle of the *why* I didn't tell you that you need to know. Even when you win the battle and you do the right things for the right reasons, some people will declare you the loser of that battle. There will be those who don't, or won't, or can't have the same influence you have, and because of their insecurities and jealousies, they will trash your motives, your work, and your service to other people.

That's okay. Not okay as in it's appropriate, right, or justified. But it's okay in that you have to let them be who they're going to be and do what they're going to do and not be distracted. The Trust Protocol is a long journey that demands focus, strength, and stamina in doses you've never dreamed of. If you get down in the mud each time someone starts slinging it, you're going to wear yourself out fighting skirmishes that don't matter, and you'll be providing oxygen to arguments that will burn out quicker if you ignore them.

Never spend a minute of time defending your motives. Spend hours testing them against Scripture, in prayer, and with godly counsel, but don't worry about defending them. Your friends don't need you to, and your enemies won't believe you.

Living out the Trust Protocol will be difficult enough if you do it right.

Guaranteed.

3

The Revolution
Will Not Be Sanitized

Embracing Messiness

The middle is messy, but it's also where the magic
happens.

Brené Brown, *Rising Strong*

My wife, Julie, is a world-class mom. She has an innate gifting when it comes to parenting that is really
something to behold. Presented with any particular
situation or circumstance requiring off-the-cuff wisdom or
discernment, she instantaneously processes an algorithm
that factors in our kids' needs in the moment, their overall
developmental maturity, and the situational context, and then
responds reflexively with the right answer. I'm typically still
trying to understand what just happened while she's already
moved on to the next thing.

And it's not only in life skills and teachable moments where she excels. One time when our children were still in the car seat phase of life, we were all together in the car when our son, Joseph, said very matter-of-factly from his car seat, "Mom . . . I don't feel so good." With no further warning, he started to throw up. Before I could pull over, find a bag, or respond in any way at all, Julie wheeled around from her passenger seat and reached back with her bare hands to catch whatever was coming up.

I've thought about that moment often since then, and I think it's a perfect illustration of the job of parenting. I don't mean that parenting as a whole is like cleaning up vomit, but when you sign up for parenting—or marriage, or following Christ, or joining a team, or a new job—you have absolutely no idea what circumstances and situations will challenge, strain, and test that relationship. If you did have access to that information prior to making the commitment, you may not make that commitment. But you commit to people and to the work to be someone who builds trust.

Building trust happens on two parallel tracks: character and competency. The trustworthiness of our character is tested every single day in myriad ways: the degree to which our walk parallels our talk, how well we deliver on what we promise, our kindness and generosity of spirit toward the people around us, how well and genuinely we encourage people, our perseverance in the face of long odds and un-expected challenges, our work ethic. These and many other factors serve as the foundation for the Trust Protocol.

While a strong foundation is essential to a sound structure, it is only the foundation. To actually impact people's lives and join in Christ's redemptive conspiracy demands productivity;

you must also demonstrate high moral character, trustworthiness, faithfulness, and dependability. Those who go by the name Christ follower have to be more than just nice people. We are created by God, for God, and called by God to do something significant in this life he's given us. So it's incumbent upon us to develop the talents and to hone the skills that actually add value to people's lives and the world around us.

David Robinson received an appointment to the US Naval Academy at Annapolis and was a standout basketball player for the Midshipmen. At 7'1", what he lacked in submarine suitability he more than made up for in athletic ability. He went on to a Hall of Fame career with the San Antonio Spurs and was named one of the 50 Greatest Players in NBA History.

Robinson's faith, his commitment to his family, and the impact he's made—particularly in the lives of San Antonio underserved youth through the founding of the Carver Academy charter school—are beyond question. An NBA award in Robinson's name is presented every year to a player in recognition of outstanding contributions to charity. The inscription on the trophy reads:

> *Following the standard set by NBA*
> *Legend David Robinson*
> *who improved the community piece by piece.*

David Robinson pieced together quite a résumé. But how many hours of practice did it take when no one was watching, when no one knew who David Robinson was or whether he'd be good enough to earn the salary, the prestige, and the fame? How many pickup games did he play over countless summer afternoons with no audience or crowds? How many injuries and aches and pains did he have to fight through in hotel rooms across the country in order to play enough minutes to amass the points, rebounds, and championships that helped establish San Antonio as one of the most successful franchises in the history of American sports?

Part of the inscription on the trophy named for him reads, "piece by piece." That's the grassroots nature of the Trust Protocol. It's piece by piece: one act of kindness at a time, one generous gift, encouraging word, persevering decision at a time.

Integrity is one of my favorite words in the English language. I love it not because of what it conveys, although I'm a fan of truth telling, ethical behavior, and relentlessly honest people. I love the word *integrity* because of the true meaning of the word and what it tells us about God's design and desire for us.

I am by nature a words guy, definitely not a numbers guy. But one thing I do recall from high school algebra is the word *integer*. Whether it is positive or negative, an integer represents a whole number, not a fraction. The word itself comes from a Latin word (*integer, integra, integrum*) that means "intact, whole, complete." It was also used in the ancient language in a figurative sense to mean "untainted, upright" or more literally "untouched."[1]

So a man or a woman or a student of integrity is someone who is whole and complete, uncorrupted. This is the state we were created in, to live in free and open relationship with God. But when sin entered the picture—both universally and individually in our own lives—it diminished our wholeness, our completeness before God. It's a struggle that continues to this very day. Any choice we make to cut an ethical corner, shade the truth a little in our favor, or mislead someone about who we are or what we've done erodes our integrity, our wholeness.

To live a life of integrity means, as Jesus instructed us, that our yes is yes, and our no is no. We don't need to carefully parse our language so as to hide behind the letter of the law. Instead, we are whole and complete when our walk parallels our talk, when we reflect the character and nature and bear the image of Jesus, who is the way, the truth, and the life.

After twenty-plus years of marriage, two children, planting a church, and sharing myriad challenges and victories, Julie remains the love of my life. By any standard you want to use, we are no longer young. But after all this time and all these miles together, I have a confession: I still love a good kiss. It doesn't have to be a long one packed with potential and innuendo—not that there's anything wrong with a kiss like that. But a sincere, heartfelt How-ya-doin'-I-still-love-you kiss is still a great thing.

A kiss communicates volumes, doesn't it? Think about it. A kiss indicates personal investment in the relationship and genuine affection. It even communicates a certain level of enjoyment in the relationship. After a disagreement, it may communicate a relational cease-fire and the normalization of relations. At some level, a sincere, heartfelt kiss is a very personal statement of love. With that thought in mind, look at what God says about kissing: "An honest answer is like a kiss on the lips" (Prov. 24:26).

A kiss on the lips is a very personal act. Acquaintances, especially in Europe, frequently greet one another with a kiss on the cheek, maybe even both cheeks. But to kiss someone on the lips communicates intimacy, connection, a familiarity beyond mere acquaintance.

When we deal with people honestly and forthrightly, we speak volumes about how we value them as people. That's why it cuts so deeply when someone we love and trust lies to us: they've demonstrated that their own comfort or gain, or whatever their reason for the deceit, was more important to them than us.

Most of us would freely acknowledge that out-and-out lying is wrong, but we know how to carefully pick and choose our words so that if we're called to the carpet we can say indignantly, "I didn't (technically) lie!" These are the half-truths and deliberate misdirections that I call *mis-honesty*. Mis-honesty falls technically short of outright *dis*honesty, but it is still deliberately misleading. It's any shading of the truth or intentional deceit cloaked in carefully chosen words that leaves someone with a false sense of what is real and true.

In his Sermon on the Mount, Jesus described in vivid, practical detail how life works in a relationship with God. Not surprisingly, he addressed the issue of honesty and the benefits and blessings that accompany simple honesty. He said, "All you need to say is simply 'Yes' or 'No'" (Matt. 5:37a). That word *simply* is a big deal. Life is simpler, easier to navigate, and more straightforward when we don't complicate it with intentional misdirections or mis-honesties, or little white lies, and certainly not out-and-out bald-faced lies. Jesus goes on to explain that there's a very good reason why: "Anything beyond this comes from the evil one" (Matt. 5:37b).

Anything beyond this . . . Anything other than what is true and real is from Satan and not God. Anytime we choose to reject God and his principles, we choose death over life, dis*integration* (there it is again!) over completeness.

Here's the spiritual reality that underlies this ethical mandate: "[Satan] was a murderer from the beginning, not holding to the truth, for there is no truth in him. When he lies, he speaks his native language, for he is a liar and the father of lies" (John 8:44). When we lie or shade the truth or intentionally mislead someone, we're speaking a foreign language, the native language of Spiritual Enemy Number One.

We were created in the spiritual and relational image of God. Part of what that means is that we're created to be truth tellers. Anything less than complete, relentless honesty is morally wrong. As far back as the Ten Commandments, we're told, "You must not testify falsely against your neighbor" (Exod. 20:16 NLT). Then Jesus says, "All you need to say is simply 'Yes' or 'No.'" In addition to the moral argument, there are strong *practical* arguments to be made in favor of relentless honesty.

Honesty Is Easier

Honesty is just plain easier. That may sound rather self-serving, but let's be honest, it's real. If you tell the truth, it is easier. Here is why:

> Send out your light and your truth;
> > let them guide me.
> Let them lead me to your holy mountain,
> > to the place where you live. (Ps. 43:3 NLT)

Truth serves not only the purposes of God and the people we seek to influence through the Trust Protocol, it also serves *us* better. When we anchor our lives to truth, we are more closely aligned with Jesus, the Truth. You and I have the ability and the opportunity to shade reality and cut ethical corners when it suits our interests. God *cannot* cut those corners, shade reality, or mislead. It is not in his character or nature to tell a lie.

When we live in relentless truth, we represent more accurately the God who created us. When we represent the God who created us, who gave us this life, this life works better. It's just easier to tell the truth.

Honesty Is More Effective

You accomplish more when you are honest. You get more stuff done. "Truthful lips endure forever, but a lying tongue lasts only a moment" (Prov. 12:19).

Think right now in your mind's eye about somebody you know who engages in dishonesty on a regular basis. We all know people like this and have to navigate these waters from time to time. The second something comes out of their mouth, we're immediately skeptical about what they've told us because they have a track record of being dishonest. Dealing with them is always more complicated than it has to be because we have to weigh their words more carefully than we do the people we know we can trust.

Truth wins out every single time because that is part of the way God has wired this world as the author of truth. It may take awhile for truth to win out, but truth will win the day. Justice will be served because honesty is more effective. It's more efficient. Think about it. If we engage in a little white lie, then we're going to burn a fair amount of mental calories remembering what we said, to whom we said it, when we said it, and what the story was so that we don't go back and step on our own mis-honesties. We've all done it. It's exhausting.

Honesty is frequently not as convenient, but it *always* works better over time.

Honesty Is Liberating

Relentless truth telling puts the wind at your back and frees you to move, live, and love freely and with abandon. "To the Jews who had believed him, Jesus said, 'If you hold to my teaching, you are really my disciples. Then you will know the truth, and the truth will set you free'" (John 8:31–32). That freedom and that abandon are going to come in real handy because there are going to be moments, days, or even seasons when we will think to ourselves, *This is too hard. I'm tired of doing the right thing and taking the high road all the time.*

Long before Kendrick Lamar, there was Gil Scott-Heron. In the early '70s, political, social, racial, and generational tensions roiled American culture from sea to shining sea. Students protested and parents panicked as seismic, tectonic shifts rattled the foundations of the country. A full generation before the earliest hints of hip-hop or rap came along, Scott-Heron was merging soul and funk music with beat poetry to capture the mood and meaning of those turbulent years.

Scott-Heron is most widely remembered for his 1971 anthem, "The Revolution Will Not Be Televised," describing the cultural upheaval that was spreading across college campuses and throughout the country as a whole. In this song, he appropriates superficial advertising slogans of the day to contrast the deeper cultural rifts rippling through the country. He punctuates each verse with the warning, "The revolution will not be televised."[2] It couldn't be prepackaged for TV, ignored, or swept under the rug of comfortable consumerism.

For all of the promise and potential of the Trust Protocol—and the glaringly attractive objective of living, working, and loving in trust—it carries with it a similar warning: the trust revolution will not be sanitized. Trust is always a messy proposition. Whether it's in a marriage or the marketplace, in the classroom or the locker room, trust always involves imperfect people with predispositions to the preservation and protection of self. And whenever people bring their own predispositions, presuppositions, motivations, and expectations to the table, we can know beyond any doubt that things can—and often will—get messy. And yet, the Trust Protocol beckons us to willingly choose to be vulnerable and to open ourselves to relational risk.

There will be those who abandon integrity and truthfulness, and they will contribute to the chaos and confusion that continue to afflict our world. But God has provided a promise that will fuel our personal commitment to truth telling, integrity, and zero tolerance for even the slightest mis-honesty in our lives. When God says, "Truthful lips endure forever, but a lying tongue lasts only a moment" (Prov. 12:19), he guarantees an enduring legacy that no dishonesty, mis-honesty, or any deception could ever hope to match.

Truth wins. Before the buzzer sounds and the cosmic game clock reaches 00:00, truth will prevail, and all the bankruptcy of all deception, falsehood, and fraud will be revealed.

Until then, though, Jesus has commanded us to be innocent as doves and shrewd as snakes, because he has sent us out as sheep among wolves.

And sometimes, the wolf is at our very door.

4

The Gift of Betrayal

Leveraging the Pain of Broken Trust

On July 7, 2000, General Tommy Franks was named Commander of CENTCOM, the US military's working group responsible for US military operations throughout Asia and the volatile Middle East. In the afternoon hours of September 11, 2001, General Franks and his wife, Cathy, were in Crete en route to Pakistan from Washington, DC. They were resting in their hotel room when an aide knocked on his door and alerted him to turn on the TV. CNN was broadcasting images of the first World Trade Tower billowing smoke against a bright blue Manhattan morning sky.

The next day, once military air traffic was cleared to land in the United States, General Franks and his staff reversed course and headed to Tampa (CENTCOM's base) to begin developing plans to dismantle the Taliban in Afghanistan.

Ten years after 9/11, after overseeing combat operations in Afghanistan and Iraq and retiring from active service in 2003, he established the General Tommy Franks Leadership Institute and Museum near his ranch in rural Oklahoma. Through a mutual friend, we invited the general to speak at our annual Spur Leadership Conference in Austin. Several months after this initial meeting, I had the opportunity to interview him for a series of leadership videos that we were capturing for Spur Leadership. I prepared for the interview as though we would talk for two hours, as opposed to the forty-five minutes we would have together in a hotel conference room.

As I was putting the finishing touches on my notes, I asked Julie what she thought I should ask him. She thought for a second, and said, "Ask him about betrayal."

The next day, we met General Franks at the appointed time and went through the interview, following the scripted questions I had prepared and a few stray thoughts he brought up on leadership challenges I hadn't known about or expected. As our time was winding down, I said to him, "General Franks, in a career as long as yours, I'm sure you had occasion to experience betrayal at some point."

His eyes lit up like he had been hit with an electrical shock, and he replied, "Oh, yes."

I said, "Talk a little about how you process that personally and how you handle that as a leader when it happens."

He began, "Mac," and then paused, measuring his words carefully. "There's only been one perfect leader in this world. And I am not him. And he experienced betrayal at a level I cannot imagine. If *he* would be betrayed, who am I to think it shouldn't or wouldn't happen to me?"

For this four-star general to process his own experiences with betrayal through the lens of Jesus's betrayal was a monster wake-up call. General Franks's insights into betrayal and the wisdom of how he processed those betrayals were *critical* in my wading through the betrayals that we had experienced. The message that God gave me through General Franks was, "This is just part of the cost of leadership and being part of the human race" (God sometimes has to speak very directly to me).

The question Julie fed me the night before that interview was born out of a season of ministry that, had that option been available, we would have dodged at all costs. Along with thirteen other people, we founded Lake Hills Church in an elementary cafetorium in the fall of 1997. For the first couple of years we worked, prayed, scraped, and cobbled together an actual church family whom we loved and enjoyed. When we moved our weekend services into Westlake High School just west of downtown Austin, the church was viable and self-sustaining.

A year later we hired one or two staff members when we started seeing some noticeable growth and began reaching people who were not "into church" at all. We were realizing the calling God had given us to redefine church for the city of Austin and beyond. And with continued growth, we added staff to serve and lead and grow what God was doing. The years between 2003 and 2010 brought significant growth as God took us from a fledgling church of two to three hundred to a congregation of more than two thousand and through the purchase of our own property and the construction of a worship center and campus.

More people meant more ministry to be shared, led, and managed. What you might not expect—and we certainly didn't—was a tectonic shift in the staff that Lake Hills Church had grown up with. With the benefit of hindsight and a great deal of prayer, I can see now that this shift was good. Even so, it was not all fun. Most of the transitions, as individuals left to pursue a new call from God, were handled in phenomenal, God-honoring ways—aboveboard, direct, honest, and with a sincere desire to honor God and bless the Lake Hills Church family.

One of those transitions led to the birth of a new church plant that we enthusiastically supported personally, spiritually, and financially. Other staff members left in complete integrity. One launched his own business; another took a position at a church in a different city. These changes were tough to navigate personally, but they were less complicated because the people involved left in ways that helped the church, and the church helped them. Win-win.

But we also felt the bite of betrayal during this season in ways that we never imagined or expected. We saw team members leave to start new churches and secretly recruit members to leave with them and support them financially. Friends and colleagues who had looked us in the eye and promised they would never do that, proceeded to do exactly that.

It's significant to note that we have always had strong relationships and friendships with other churches and pastors in our hometown. We believe deeply in the fact that God raises up different churches for different purposes, and that it is part of his creative, redemptive genius. We celebrate and honor that. But to secretly plan and work to plant one church while still being paid by another, and to actively recruit members of that church and lie about it—that's a different animal altogether. It creates confusion, doubt, and uncertainty that is avoidable. By the time I sat down with General Franks in that hotel conference room, we had been through a gauntlet of betrayal and deceit.

Yet, I wouldn't trade it for a thing. Between a couple of those waves of loss and betrayal, Hebrews 10:24—the "love and good deeds" foundation for the Trust Protocol—struck me in such a profound, fresh way that it radically altered the trajectory of every relationship I have and everything I think about and participate in—my marriage, my parenting, and my leadership.

We've always had a young staff, and many of them, like Julie and me, were surprised and more than slightly discouraged that friends and colleagues would leave, particularly in the way that some did. As the pastor, especially to our staff, I was grasping for handles, not only to process all the changes those departures sparked but also to process it all personally. That's when I decided that "love and good deeds" would be ground zero for us. If we could weather that season loving each other—*trusting* each other—and still maintain a healthy sense of urgency and productivity in our ministries, then we would come out on the other side of those betrayals not only surviving but actually thriving.

The Trust Protocol answered the *what* question: *What would be our goal and our model to follow?* Answer: *Love and good deeds.* The *how* question would prove to be a much bigger and more difficult one to answer.

Betrayal is the greatest personal pain a person can endure. All others pale in comparison because they are less personal and less purposeful. The only person who can betray us is someone we've chosen to trust who has chosen to break that trust. When that trust is deliberately and purposefully destroyed, we have to decide how we are going to respond.

Actually, it's more accurate to say that we *get* to decide how to respond, because in our response to betrayal we can strike a massive vein of hope, like a ribbon of gold that lies undiscovered for centuries but is stumbled upon and mined for everything it's worth. My personal discovery of this spiritual gold mine was not a linear path. To be completely candid, it took longer than I like to admit, and it certainly took longer than I wish it had.

I'm not proud of the fact that it took me as long as it did to get past that season, and it's painful to recall—and certainly not easy to share here. But I hope our story can serve as a springboard in your story when you encounter betrayal. Whenever you decide to participate in the Trust Protocol, do so with your eyes wide open and realize that it likely means you will be betrayed. Someone will choose to not reciprocate your trust and will refuse whatever it is you're offering: friendship, a business partnership, romance, a lifetime commitment, a trust-based working relationship, church membership—whatever. Whenever we choose to trust, we always run the risk of betrayal.

I was incredibly blessed to be surrounded by a phenomenal, godly wife; amazing friends who provided wise, godly counsel and encouragement; and an extraordinary church family, in addition to the aid of a gifted Christian counselor who helped me process my emotions and work through the *process* of forgiveness.

Sometimes, forgiveness is an event. If the offense suffered is small enough, we can forgive and move on in a relatively quick manner. Other times, though, forgiveness comes at a much higher cost. Forgiveness frequently has to be a repeated, conscious choice to abandon the resentment and pain caused by someone's betrayal. Forgiveness does not require re-trusting that person, but it does require the conscious releasing of any bitterness, contempt, or disdain for the other person, regardless of whether or not they acknowledge the wrong.

Because we are at our core relational creatures and because our relationships can be damaged, volumes have been written about forgiveness. Forgiveness forms the basis for the restoration of our relationship with God that was ruptured by our sin. But one thing in particular not only helped me process the betrayal and choose to forgive more quickly and completely but also radically altered the way I was forgiving.

When I explained the situation to the counselor I was meeting with, he took it all in, made some notes, and then said, "Wow. That's a lot. I want you to know that it makes sense to me that you're having trouble moving past this."

Relieved to hear him say that, I said, "Thanks . . . I was kinda hoping I wasn't blowing this out of proportion."

He said, "No, not at all. I think it's important for you to know beyond a shadow of a doubt that you did not deserve that. No one does. You did not deserve to be treated like that. You didn't deserve any better than that, but you sure didn't deserve that."

I was halfway into my next question, when I mentally skidded to a stop (*insert screeching tires sound*). I thought to myself, *I'm paying for this so let's get all our money's worth outta this one.* I said, "Um . . . let me back up for a second. What do you mean, I didn't deserve any better than that?"

He asked, "What do you mean?"

I said, "Okay, let's take me out of this. I would say that you deserve to be treated with respect and dignity and honesty because you're a child of God. Wouldn't you?"

Calmly, he responded, "No, I wouldn't." And then he delivered the punch line that changed everything. "I would say I'm *worthy* of those things—because I'm created in the image of God and because of what God says about who I am—but that doesn't mean I *deserve* them. When I assume I deserve something, that means I think I'm entitled to it. And entitlement is a cancer to myself and every relationship that I'm in."

That was a particularly bitter pill to swallow for me, because I had identified entitlement as central to the betrayals we had experienced. But as I processed through that session and prayed over my response to the whole ordeal, I realized that the key to my truly forgiving and moving on was embedded in his counsel.

Worthiness—of love, respect, trust, or any of the good things we crave and receive in our relationships—is chemotherapy to the cancer of entitlement. When we realize that we are worthy of certain gifts and blessings because of who God says we are, we understand that our worthiness flows out of his amazing grace. He created us. He sustains us. He provides for us. He protects us. He disciplines us. He loves us. Exactly none of those things is due to anything we have done or deserve. They are all expressions of his grace.

We are worthy—of love, respect, honesty, and trust—because he has endowed us with a divine dignity, so we perceive everything through the lens of his grace. From the air we breathe, to the blessings we enjoy, to the challenges we endure—they are all vehicles of his grace. So we no longer view the world through the lenses of what we are owed, or deserve, or are entitled to.

Nowhere is this more evident than in the earthly life of Jesus. If anyone could assume he was owed respect and deference, it would be the Son of God. And, to be sure, as Cocreator, Savior, and Lord, he is due all our praise. But over and over again he was ridiculed, mocked, ignored, plotted against, threatened, and betrayed. Yet there is not one instance of his being offended or defensive about his ministry, his role, or his credentials as the Messiah.

He regularly rebuked and corrected the Pharisees. He drove the money changers out of the temple. But it was not because he was offended or insulted. It was always because of the danger to other people's perceptions of the kingdom of God or the prostitution of the temple for financial gain. Jesus never forfeited his worthiness as the Son of God, but neither did he ever assume any entitlement.

Our God-ordained worthiness is the key that unlocks the door to forgiveness and the capacity to trust other people again, even after our trust has been betrayed and broken. This revelation can anchor our minds and hearts through the pain, anger, and bewilderment of betrayal. But it won't solve the problem all by itself. Reconciling all those emotions and returning to the land of the living requires a deep-seated resolve and grit and commitment to a process that may need to be repeated in order to take root and bear fruit.

Acknowledge the Pain

First, we need to acknowledge the pain. This may seem obvious, but too often in our attempt to escape the pain of betrayal, we fail to adequately acknowledge the depth or the degree of the pain of betrayal. As I've opened up to friends and asked around, I've discovered the universal distribution of betrayal. Everyone who has trusted has experienced betrayal on some level. The only difference among us is how thoroughly we managed to process our personal stories of betrayal.

When General Franks said, "Who am I to think it shouldn't or wouldn't happen to me?," it was a powerful, spiritually convicting moment. What I heard the Lord say to me in his grace and love and truth was the same thing I heard through General Franks: "Suck it up, Buttercup." In other words, this is part of it. If you trust, if you love, if you lead, you will be betrayed. And the sooner you acknowledge that, the sooner you will be able to get through it and move past it to do what you need to do, to love whom you need to love, to be who you need to be.

Acknowledging the pain requires a certain level of humility to admit that we have been duped. I like to think of myself as somewhat discerning, but when we were so deeply deceived, I had to admit that I had been very wrong about some people, people I loved and still love, people I had trusted, people I had endorsed and supported. Recognizing that and admitting it to myself and those closest to me were absolutely necessary to be able to do something about the pain.

Address the Pain

Second, we need to address the pain. Everyone processes differently. Some people process pain and disappointment quickly, while others chew on it, replay it, and rehash it over and over ad nauseum. For me, I literally could not process it. I couldn't figure out what to do with the experience or the reality that we were dealing with. And since I couldn't process it and put it into a neat, organized filing system in my brain,

I kept churning the experience and the emotions associated with it. That churning is what led me to seek counseling.

I love to fish, especially fly-fishing for tarpon in the Florida Keys. Now, I know that from April to June, tarpon migrate and congregate in massive numbers around Islamorada, Marathon, and all the way down to Key West. But the guides who fish those waters every day know where the fish move from day to day, what the tides are doing hour by hour, the weather that changes from minute to minute, and the moon phase that affects everything from their spawning to worm hatches that send them into a feeding frenzy. The algorithms that the guides compute minute to minute and hour to hour determine whether or not the angler will see fish to cast to.

A good counselor is like a good fishing guide. They understand the basics of human emotions and psychological processing, but they can also help us see things objectively. We are frequently too close to a situation to see it clearly in order to address the pain, or the uncertainty, or whatever it is that is tripping us up.

Other key players in addressing the pain are the true friends we have in our lives. I'm not sure where Julie and I would be had we not had the relentless support of friends and family like Ed and Lisa Young and David and Lisa Hughes through that season and every season since. Their counsel and comfort—and laughter and loyalty!—were critical and literally heaven-sent at a time when we desperately needed them. They were there to offer support and course-correct our thinking from time to time to help get us where God wanted us to be. There were a lot of late-night conversations and cross-country phone calls that played a massive role in our healing.

Abandon the Pain

Lastly, we need to abandon the pain. Through the years, God has blessed us with incredible friends and resources for insights and friendships in ministry across the country. Bil Cornelius and his wife, Jessica, pastor Church Unlimited in Corpus Christi with campuses throughout south Texas. One day during that season of betrayal, Bil asked me how I was doing, and I told him what we were dealing with. Without a breath of hesitation, he responded, "Don't stay hurt too long."

In that moment, I thought, *That's a good word*, and I told Bil so. In the following months and years, I realized just how wise and insightful that advice was. *Don't stay hurt too long.* It's one thing to *be* hurt. It's entirely another to *stay* hurt.

We can't control when we are hurt. But we do determine in large measure how long we stay hurt. Some injuries take longer to heal than others. When I was a kid, I broke my leg twice. The first time was a serious fracture, both bones just above the ankle, clean through. I spent two months in a full leg cast, followed by a month in a cast to the knee. The second time, I barely chipped my tibia just as it enters the ankle and was out of the cast in six weeks.

To abandon the pain is the fruit of forgiveness. It's the payoff of a pardon. Forgiveness frees us up to move past the pain, no matter how deep, no matter how real. This is why forgiveness is something we do for ourselves and not for the person we're forgiving.

This is the chapter that almost never was. I really debated whether to include it for several reasons. I wasn't sure that I really wanted to wade through all the emotions and memories from that season again. We have processed—acknowledged, addressed, and abandoned the pain—we have forgiven, and we have moved on. I also don't like to give that time and those memories too much oxygen. I had allowed it to be a distraction longer than it should have been, and I don't want to let that happen ever again.

But betrayal is an absolutely guaranteed residual of the Trust Protocol. When we build trust, give trust, and look for it in return, we will be betrayed. And yet, we rarely discuss it or read about it or learn how to process something that is universally experienced. If we don't acknowledge, address, and abandon the pain of betrayal, it can stall the engine of trust so completely that we never crank it up again.

What a tragedy it would be if we allowed our painful, negative experiences to override our hope and choke out our belief in the possibility and potential of what God is calling us to. That's why this chapter is titled "The Gift of Betrayal." In the midst of our season of betrayal—and others since then, by the way—there were shoots of green grass of God's grace sprouting up in the desert. God regularly reminded me, "Look around and see who *hasn't* betrayed you."

As we absorbed the body blows of betrayal, God's faithfulness was present and powerful in the loyalty and love of those who stayed—so many of our staff and the committed, faithful members of our church family. Their support, friendship, love, and presence helped us abandon the pain we felt and move past it into the next season God had already prepared for us.

They were the ones who showed us that what matters most are relationships.

5

It's the Relationship, Stupid

The Foundation of Everything That Lasts

In the summer of 1991, President George Herbert Walker Bush was enjoying approval ratings of historic proportions. Having served as vice president in the Reagan administration, director of the CIA, ambassador to China, congressman, and multiple political appointments dating back to the sixties, he was most celebrated as commander-in-chief during the brief but highly successful Gulf War of 1990–91. To ensure victory in that conflict, he forged a worldwide coalition of nations led by the United States that successfully expelled Sadam Hussein's Iraqi army from neighboring Kuwait, and he led the execution of the exit strategy once the war was won.

Nine months later, he was voted out of office.

President Bush's tenure was ended by the election of a young Southern Democrat named Bill Clinton. It was a reversal of fortune, almost as shocking in its velocity as in the actual result. To be sure, Clinton's election marked a departure in American politics: he was the first baby boomer elected president on a ticket of unlikely geographical and demographic similarities, as he and Al Gore both hail from southern states and were both relatively young. The unlikely upset was orchestrated by a driven, hard-charging Cajun named James Carville. Carville cut his political teeth in the cutthroat politics and backwoods bayous of Louisiana, honing his instincts and claws for a presidential campaign of just this ilk.

Early on, Carville identified a flagging US economy as a vulnerable Achilles' heel of the Bush campaign. In every Clinton campaign office around the country, signs went up that read, IT'S THE ECONOMY, STUPID. Everyone, from the candidate to the most junior-level volunteer staffer, was expected to remain focused—and to refocus the electorate's attention—on the nation's economic challenges. By the time election day rolled around, they had successfully cast their candidate as the choice most likely to help not only the American economy but also actual Americans themselves. Everything in the campaign revolved around the admittedly harsh reminder: IT'S THE ECONOMY, STUPID.

Where the Trust Protocol is practiced, a similar single-mindedness serves us well: it's the relationship, stupid. I know, I know—it's not a particularly sweet or kind reminder, but the fact is, we frequently lose focus on what matters most. We forget that God created us in his image as relational beings and that we have soul-deep, God-given relational needs in every single endeavor or enterprise we enter into. And what matters most is people. It's easy to lose sight of this and focus on and manage the externals and the measurables at the expense of people, who instinctively bristle at being *managed* like an inanimate object.

No relationship brings this nonnegotiable principle into sharper focus than the bond between parents and their children. For millennia, parents have searched in vain for assurance, a guarantee, or some promise that if we check the right parenting boxes we can know that our kids will turn out all right. A funny thing happened on the way to perfect parenting, though: kids! (Okay, and we parents aren't perfect either.)

But those pesky kids get a voice in how things turn out in their lives. It's a voice that grows as they go from complete and utter dependence on their parents for survival to deciding how much weight they'll give their parents' voices in their decision making. Parents begin forging credibility with their children at birth. Before they're even aware of it, our children learn that they can count on us for food, cleaning, cuddling, pain relief, love, comfort, and all the other things we provide.

Things get more complicated from there. As they grow and mature, their needs and the right decisions become more complex and have greater consequences. The stakes grow higher at the very time they're discovering just how imperfect we can be. Mark Twain is credited with saying, "When I was a boy of fourteen, my father was so ignorant I could hardly stand to have the old man around. But when I got to be twenty-one, I was astonished at how much he had learned in seven years."

In that window of the parent-child relationship, trust can close the generation gap. During her last year of college, our daughter, Emily, gave Julie and me one of the greatest gifts we have ever received. It wasn't a thing she gave us; it was something she said in a cross-country phone call: "I didn't always like what y'all told me to do or not to do. But I always knew you were telling me for my good." Julie and I silently high-fived over that one. No need to spike the ball and do a parental touchdown dance.

Read between the lines of what Emily was really saying when she said, "I always knew you were telling me for my good." She trusted us to parent in her best interest, not ours. She and Joseph knew that we weren't disciplining or reprimanding them because of how their behavior affected us. It was about how their choices and their behavior would affect them and set them up for future success or failure.

When Emily was in high school, I tried to coax her to do her best academically, to study perhaps a little more diligently than she was. One evening when everything was calm and things were good I said to her, "Emily, let's be honest. You are a person who likes to leave your options open. You've never liked anyone making decisions for you or telling you what you can and can't do." She agreed. I continued, "The better your grades, the better your scores and recommendations from your teachers, the more options you're going to have when it comes time to go to college. And even before you get to choosing a college, the better you do and the more you take care of your business, the less Mom and I are going to tell you what to do and not to do around here because we'll see that you're handling your life well."

The point was, for Julie and me, *that Emily was the point*! And the same held true for Joseph. Julie and I never worried about our kids liking us. But we worked overtime to make sure they knew we liked them. We did that not so they would feel good about themselves, but so they knew they could trust us. We knew the day was coming—and would arrive far sooner than we wanted it to—when they would make decisions independent of us. If we could convince them we were for them and wanted only God's best for their sake, then we had a shot at forging credibility even when they didn't understand the reasons behind our rules.

Rules without relationship result in resentment. Relationship with rules results in respect. But this principle isn't restricted to parent-child relationships. Everything in life worth doing, worth pursuing, demands relationship. Whatever business, vocation, or calling we engage in, the Trust Protocol assumes that we're in the people business. We have to be able to do relationship well if we're going to do anything of value and substance well over time.

Some might point to successful football coaches or marketplace leaders or even some in ministry who put up big numbers and *appear* to be what is commonly accepted as "successful." Yet, despite their apparent successes, behind the curtain many are significantly relationally impaired or oblivious. We might ask, "What about them? They're doing just fine, and they don't have *any* true friends or real family connectedness." *If* (and I emphasize *if*) that's the case, then they have, by definition, failed the Trust Protocol.

In John 13, Jesus demands of his followers something so radical, so revolutionary, that it stands on end the dominant worldview of success and failure: "Your love for one another will prove to the world that you are my disciples" (v. 35 NLT). Not your success. Not your bank account. Not your children's behavior, your GPA or points per game, the house you live in, or the car you drive. Zero, zip, zilch, nada. Exactly *none* of the things that the world uses to measure success or personal worth count in Jesus's evaluation of our faithfulness. Just one thing does: How well do you love?

With our families and closest friends, we at least have a pretty good idea of how to love them. We certainly don't do it perfectly all the time, but we know that we should and, for the most part, how we should. Outside of those closest relationships, it can be especially difficult to discern how to represent Christ in ways that resonate with another person as well as reflect and respect the relationship with that person as it is currently constituted.

Our tendency is to drift toward one of two extremes. Either we distance ourselves too much, or we cling too closely. As a child of the '80s, I can't help but recall the vintage wisdom of the Southern rock band .38 Special who advised us, "Hold on loosely, but don't let go; if you cling too tightly, you're gonna lose control."[1] While their description is spot-on, their prescription for our predicament leaves more than a little to be desired. I think we'd be wise to instead look to Scripture for our marching orders and see what God calls us to do in loving *everyone* well.

In Romans 12, Paul is explaining in vivid detail not only the beauty and the power of the gospel, the Good News of Jesus, but also the power and beauty of living out that gospel. Here's what he says as it relates to loving well:

> Love must be sincere. Hate what is evil; cling to what is good. Be devoted to one another in love. Honor one another above yourselves. Never be lacking in zeal, but keep your spiritual fervor, serving the Lord. Be joyful in hope, patient

in affliction, faithful in prayer. Share with the Lord's people who are in need. Practice hospitality. (vv. 9–13)

First, *love must be sincere*. No-matter-what, true, Jesus-style love is real. It is sincere. It looks at everyone through the lens of *people matter to me because they matter to God and are made in his image*. So, the first thing we do is evaluate our motives concerning other people. Do we see them as expendable and replaceable resources or as sons and daughters of God?

Second, *hate what is evil; cling to what is good. Be devoted to one another in love. Honor one another above yourselves.* Okay, now we're getting down to it. To honor someone above ourselves may be the most counterintuitive, unnatural move we ever learn. Our natural inclination, the innate bent of our hearts, is toward ourselves. We are born spiritually predisposed to self-interest, self-protection, and self-promotion. To be devoted to one another in love is to choose the interests of another over our own self-interests.

To honor one another above ourselves is to be truly Christlike. Jesus said very clearly in John 15:13, "There is no greater love than to lay down one's life for one's friends" (NLT). In that declaration, he was clearly referencing his impending sacrificial, physical death on the cross. But he was also teaching us the underlying spiritual truth: love = sacrifice.

To honor others above ourselves is to lift them up, to value them more than our own self-interests, to prioritize their wants, needs, and desires above our own. This is the very definition of sacrifice. To love others or value them above ourselves if it's convenient or fits in our agenda is merely window dressing. When we value those who cannot advance our cause or grow our platform, we truly value them as God does.

Where this gets blurry is in relationships we have at work or school or on teams—basically, those relationships that *shouldn't* enjoy the familiarity or intimacy we share in our families or with our closest friends. We're not going to achieve or even desire the same intimacy with coworkers that we enjoy with family. But the Trust Protocol can still thrive and flourish at differing degrees of connectedness.

Some people will argue for transparency as the currency of trust. And to be sure, relationships such as marriage, parent-child, and others do require transparency to be everything God intends them to be. But I would argue that *most* of our relationships are not built to sustain the weight of transparency. And we shouldn't expect them to be.

What we should expect is authenticity. I can be authentic with my wife, Julie, and our kids, Emily and Joseph. But there are some conversations Julie and I have that our kids, friends, and church members don't need to know about. I'm still authentic with those other groups, but I'm not going to bare my soul to everyone. Rather than complete transparency with everyone all the time, our guiding principle should be: authentic with everyone, transparent with a precious few.

Authenticity cultivates trust in every relationship and partnership we have. The fact is, though, that not every relationship will survive, nor should they. Maybe you've hired someone who doesn't fulfill their duties. After providing feedback, course-correcting their performance, and setting clear expectations, releasing them may be necessary. Perhaps you work for someone who disrupts or damages the Trust Protocol so regularly that it's impossible to sustain the working relationship while preserving your integrity. After respectfully seeking to find common ground and doing everything in your purview to establish trust, it may mean a career change for you. Or maybe you're dating someone who doesn't meet your expectations, hopes, and prayers for a longer-term relationship. When you reach that bridge, crossing it with that person is a bridge too far and ending the relationship is necessary. In all these situations, you can absolutely still apply the Trust Protocol, even as you sever the relationship.

Getting back to Romans 12, Paul continues to pull the thread that he started in verses 9–10: "If it is possible, as far as it depends on you, live at peace with everyone" (Rom. 12:18). What an incredible command and relational life raft! First of all, the responsibility: *If it is possible . . . live at peace with everyone.* If it is at all possible, do everything you can, in the wisdom of the Holy Spirit, through the power of prayer, to live at peace. With everyone. Members of the Jesus tribe should never settle for ambivalence, animosity, or isolation from one another or those outside the family of faith. If it is possible, do everything you can to live at peace.

But there's that wonderful qualifier that the Holy Spirit breathed into Paul's Letter to the Romans: *as far as it depends on you.* One of the realities of this fallen world is that we will not be able to live at peace with everyone. There will absolutely be people in our lives who will never grow sick and tired of waking up sick and tired. Barring a miraculous intervention of the Lord, they're going to stay mad at the world and perhaps even mad at you. When you can stand before the Lord assured that you have done everything possible to reconcile the relationship, and you've confessed any wrongdoing on your part and have asked their forgiveness—if it's not forthcoming, move on. Jesus told his disciples when he sent them out on a short-term missionary expedition,

Whatever town or village you enter, search there for some worthy person and stay at their house until you leave. As you enter the home, give it your greeting. If the home is deserving, let your peace rest on it; if it is not, let your peace return to you. If anyone will not welcome you or listen to your words, leave that home or town and shake the dust off your feet. (Matt. 10:11–14)

Many times, we try to change someone's mind who has no interest in changing their mind. It's as if we think we could somehow open their cranium, deposit the thoughts and motivations we want them to have, close it back up, and then have them act on the thoughts and motivations we installed. The fact is, no matter how difficult it is to accept, all we can do is all we can do.

But that is liberating and empowering in the context of the Trust Protocol. *All I can do* actually turns out to be quite a lot. I can

- own responsibility for every word, thought, and motive that radiates out of me;
- fess up when I mess up;
- pray for opportunities to reconcile and restore relationships that I might have helped damage;
- measure my words carefully before flying off the handle;
- look for opportunities to encourage and affirm the people in my sphere of influence.

In short, I can make every effort to live in peace with those around me. When I assume appropriate relational responsibility for what I can and should do, I have then chosen to live in hope and power, and something super-natural takes place. I have created hope that things can improve or grow and develop. And I have taken action that creates and perpetuates a God-honoring, God-given power to make a difference, to make an impact, no matter the situation or circumstances. I'm no longer a spectator, passively reacting to life as it happens around me and to me. I'm now a player, a participant in the action that I'm actually a part of.

At the same time, we generate God-honoring hope and power. *All I can do* also helps us to differentiate between all we should do and all we should not do. When seeking rela-tional restoration, there are a number of misguided methods we need to make sure are not in our repertoire:

- Assuming responsibility for *all* of the problem.
- Accepting blame for things we didn't say or motives we didn't have.
- Taking responsibility for other people's choices (words, actions, and so on). I can't ever *make* anyone act a certain way, just as other people can't *make* me say or do certain things. We all make our own choices about how we respond to other people and situations.
- Taking back something we said. Once it's said, it's out there. We can apologize and sincerely ask for forgive-ness, but our words have weight. We shouldn't recklessly throw them around.
- Holding a grudge if the other person holds a grudge. Their choice to forgive is exactly that: *their choice.* We

are called to do all *we* can do, not what another person can or should do.

For a lot of people, prioritizing relationships above everything else is a scary proposition. You may be a highly driven, Type-A personality whose efficiencies, goal setting, and achievements have proved highly lucrative in the marketplace or effective in a nonprofit environment. Or perhaps relationships just don't come naturally or easily for you, so you shuttle them to the back burner and focus on performance, task management, and to-do lists. Sometimes too we just get tired of people. If you endure a season of multiple relational challenges, the last thing you want to do is wade into new waters of draining discomfort, potential pitfalls, and uncharted uncertainty.

In my own life and ministry, I've noticed a trend that is gradually but convincingly proving to be an immutable law: every time I notice a problem or a crisis that's brewing in some relationship, and I choose to ignore it or merely hope it gets better on its own without actually addressing it, it always resurfaces. And the damage then, or even just the discomfort, is always greater than if I had addressed it when I first noticed it—every single time.

Not surprisingly, when I answer the call of Romans 12 and honor people above myself and make every effort to live in peace with everyone, things work better—my marriage with Julie, our relationships with our kids, coworkers, friends, neighbors, people at my gym, *everyone*.

That's not to say everything always works out and we always end up hugging. To be sure, some people will have no interest in pursuing that kind of God-honoring, God-commanded peace. But even that, in God's economy, is a blessing. By making sure that you have done everything you could, when someone doesn't join you on the reconciliation train, you're liberated and free to move on and follow God's leading to the next adventure. You may grieve the loss of friendship or relationship, but in your grief, you can know the peace of God that passes understanding and have the confidence that comes from a clean heart.

If it is possible . . . You have to try.

6

You Have to Try!

Taking a Shot against All Odds

Christmas is a big deal. Obviously, the birth of our Lord ranks as a monumental observance every year, but in this context, I mean it is huge in our family. My wife, Julie, inherited from her father a deep love of all things noel, and her enthusiasm infuses our home with passion and excitement for Christmas all year long.

Once we finish Christmas Eve services at Lake Hills Church in Austin, our family heads for Mississippi to visit Julie's family, unwind, eat too much, hunt, and generally decompress after the holiday frenzy. It's a time that we target every year, and it recharges our batteries for the approaching new year.

Every morning during this break, some of us will fan out into the woods deer hunting, seeking to provide protein and sustenance for our loved ones—it's a tough job, but someone has to do it. Once the hunters come in from the field and the teenagers are crawling out of bed, midmorning usually finds the entire family gathered in the kitchen sharing bacon and eggs, biscuits, and coffee amid loud, raucous, and frequently entertaining conversations.

One year recently, Julie and her sisters were discussing a family friend who has struggled for years with diabetes and other weight-related health issues. Overhearing their conversation, my father-in-law, Joe, interjected the following: "Well . . . I'm about to talk to her and tell her I'm going to help her get that lap-band surgery so she won't eat so much."

Julie and her sisters looked back at him blankly, completely baffled as to how to respond. Personally, I was just so incredibly grateful that I was present to see how this particular family discussion would play out. Finally, Julie said, "Dad! You can't say that to her!"

Joe replied, "What? Why not?"

Julie, still stunned, said, "Dad, you can't tell a woman that she needs lap-band surgery because of her weight!"

"Julie, I can't let her die!"

"But you can't say *that* to her." At this point, Julie's mom and two sisters joined in the chorus to help her make this same point to Joe.

Undeterred, Joe said passionately, "Girls . . . Kathy . . . when someone is harming themselves, you cannot just sit by and watch. *You have to do something.*" And then, with growing passion and emotion, he said, "*You have to try!*"

Horrified, Julie and her mom and sisters realized that they were not going to sway Joe from his conviction that he had to try to help their friend, so they abandoned their efforts to change his mind. I don't know what became of that proposed conversation between Joe and their family friend, but I do know that Julie and I have returned repeatedly in our marriage and in ministry to the mantra, *You have to try!*

So often, we anticipate and predict people's response to a hard conversation or an accountability question and decide that they won't receive it well, or they won't respond honestly, or they'll blow up and dig their heels in, or they'll have some other negative response. And in the light of this hypothetical, completely fabricated prediction, we choose to avoid the hard conversations or the tough questions. But the Trust Protocol does not afford us this luxury.

We have to be willing to enter into these conversations precisely because we *do* love people. And the more we love them, the more closely and intimately we're connected to them, the more penetrating and personal the conversations are going to be. One of the great challenges and joys of marriage is being willing to initiate or receive a hard conversation for the purpose of changing behavior, recalibrating the relationship, and restoring it to a solid footing.

Early in our marriage, Julie and I really struggled to find common ground in one particular area. Whenever we broached this subject or it reared its ugly head, we instinctively danced around it or hydroplaned over it hoping we could escape before we had to really dig in and tackle it. We were young and in love and loved being married, but this one area was a minefield of emotion and sensitive feelings that we knew to avoid.

One day, soon after our daughter, Emily, was born, the subject surfaced again. Before I knew it, Julie's eyes welled up with tears, and she said, "I don't want to live like this. I think we need to go see a counselor." In that moment, though we had only been married three years, I knew that even if we stayed married, avoiding this issue wasn't a long-term solution for our marriage to be everything God wanted it to be.

You have to try.

On the morning of our first appointment, we walked into the lobby of the counselor's office, and Julie ran her finger down the office directory to find where we needed to go. I remember thinking, *Don't do that! Someone may see what office we're looking for and think we're crazy!* I didn't say it out loud, but I thought it.

Sitting in his office and sharing our story with that Christian counselor, I realized that Julie and I were absolutely on the same team. This was not a me versus her issue; this was an *us* issue. We needed to figure out how to process it and how to get on the same page with the same goals, despite our very different personalities and backgrounds. What I had feared would be an exercise in navel-gazing futility actually proved to affirm and reinforce our marriage and remind us that we really were on the same team. In this particular area, we just had to discover how to act like we were and to behave toward one another like we wanted and had committed to.

You have to try.

For years, I have admired, studied, and marveled at Winston Churchill. Anyone who can save the world from fascist tyranny while smoking Cuban cigars is worthy, I think, of our gratitude and admiration. Something he said speaks directly and uniquely to this idea of grit. Historians are divided over the exact origin of the quote, but it is almost certainly born out of World War II during Germany's near-constant bombardment of Great Britain: "It is not enough that we do our best; sometimes we must do what is required."[1]

Sometimes in our relationships—at work, at home, in the neighborhood, at school—we can feel as though we are under bombardment. Constant shelling with the threat of more to come can drive us underground to our relational bunkers like the Brits went into the shelters of the London metro system, the Tube. We tire of trying and decide that it's just not worth it. Sometimes we detonate a bomb ourselves. More often, we let the connection wear and fray from disrepair until both parties decide it's beyond fixing. We might even say, "We did everything we could" or "We just grew apart" or some variation of those themes.

Many factors affect our willingness to try to engage in relational repair or accountability conversations. For a lot of us, many of them happen at a subterranean emotional and psychological level we're not even aware of, but the consequences and results of these factors can still surface and wreak relational havoc in our homes, businesses, and other communities we participate in. The factors included here are not an exhaustive list, and they are certainly not intended to be exhausting. Rather, they are presented simply to raise awareness and identify some of the bad actors that frequently torpedo our willingness to dig in, engage, and reinforce or repair our relationships. You have to try.

Inexperience. Often we don't make the effort to mend a ruptured relationship because we simply don't know how. Much of what we do relationally flows out of what we acquire along the way, particularly from our families of origin. The household and the families we grow up in affect us in ways we're not even aware of.

When Julie and I got married, we came from polar opposite family situations. My parents were divorced; hers are still married today. I have two brothers; she has two sisters. She grew up in small-town Mississippi; I grew up in suburban Houston.

My brothers and I could argue, disagree, sometimes even physically fight each other and minutes later be playing video games or playing outside like nothing had ever happened. Imagine my surprise when I married Julie and discovered that not everyone grew up where you could say whatever came into your mind, then apologize and move on like nothing had ever happened. Let's just say that Julie did not share the same philosophy of conflict resolution that my brothers and I had spent a lifetime perfecting.

If I said something hurtful or harsh, it did not go away easily or quickly. I had to learn how to say things in a way that was honest but not quite as forceful as I had learned growing up with brothers. It wasn't that I wanted to communicate harshly or didn't care about her feelings. I did care deeply. I just didn't know how to communicate with kindness.

Fatigue. Sometimes we fail to engage in hard conversations because we're simply too tired: tired from work, tired from people, tired of being back in relational repair mode again, tired of dealing with the same issue over and over and over again. Vince Lombardi famously said, "Fatigue makes cowards of us all."[2] While coach-speak may be a little off-putting for some, the fact is, he was right.

When I'm tired, whether in the moment or in a season of life, my tendency is to avoid confrontation. My courage fades. There have been times when Julie, out of the blue, would ask me a question about a challenge at church or a leadership trial we're facing, and I've replied (lovingly, I'm sure), "I just can't do that right now. I'm out of gas." Depending on the issue, that answer is temporarily acceptable, but it falls far short of adequate over time. Sometimes you have to address the issue regardless of how tired you may be.

This struggle seems to surface most frequently in the context of parenting. No matter what you do for a living or where you're engaged vocationally, nothing is as 24/7 constant as parenting, *if* you're paying attention and in the game. I vividly remember times during the years that Emily and Joseph were growing up when I would see a teachable moment, a parentable moment, and choose to look the other way, or I would ignore something just because I was tired. I was largely cured of this when I noticed a disturbing trend: every single time I hoped something would get better or their choices would improve without addressing the issue—and I mean, every single time—it resurfaced. Without fail, unresolved issues return, typically larger and angrier than the previous time.

Laziness. Sometimes we don't tackle relational challenges because we just don't feel like it. We know what the issue is. We know we ought to do something or say something, but in the moment, it's just easier not to.

We fear the response—backlash, anger, indifference, cold shoulder, and so on. But what we have to remember is that the danger of chronic passivity far outweighs the danger of acute discomfort triggered by a sincere desire to restore trust and recalibrate the relationship.

My first car was a 1975 Toyota Celica. I bought it when I turned sixteen in 1982. A couple years later, the brakes began squeaking ever so slightly when I came to a stop. It was so slight and came on so gradually that I barely noticed. Then the squeaking became more pronounced, and there was no doubt that it emanated from my car and not someone else's at a light or stop sign. But by then, I was used to it, so I rolled merrily along.

Until . . . the squeaking became a grinding. Apparently, when one allows one's brakes to deteriorate badly enough, the pads wear down to the point that the caliper begins to literally grind into the rotor where it grabs the wheel to slow the car down. Who knew! What should have cost well under one hundred dollars became a major repair costing multiple hundreds of dollars, all because I didn't address the issue when it was minor.

How much more expensive relationally, professionally, or parentally when we allow problems to deteriorate unchecked and unaddressed until the cost to repair the relationship appears too high to pay, until *it would take too long and hurt too much*.

Growing up in Houston, my childhood was *Leave It to Beaver*-esque. My brothers and I played T-ball and basketball and freely roamed our neighborhood on our banana-seat Schwinn bicycles, like suburban *Sons of Anarchy*. Mom and Dad made sure that we were at church every Sunday where they both taught Sunday school and Dad was a deacon. I had confessed my sins, trusted Christ, and gotten baptized in second grade. My dad put on a suit and tie and went to work every morning, commuting to what was then the Tenneco building downtown while my mom held down the fort at home for my brothers and me. Mom never vacuumed wearing pearls like June, but we were basically the Cleavers.

Until we weren't.

One Sunday afternoon in 1979 when I was in the seventh grade, my brothers and I were watching the Houston Oilers and Cincinnati Bengals play in overtime. Our parents told us we needed to talk and to turn off the TV. I knew it was serious when we had to turn off an overtime game.

I don't remember the exact words or even how long the conversation lasted, but I remember the net effect: my dad was leaving and moving out. I remember my mom saying through her tears, "Tom, please don't," over and over before he walked out the door carrying an overnight bag and his Bible. I still don't know how I knew it, but I knew that afternoon, at twelve years old, that he wasn't coming back, that our family had just splintered and life as we knew it was over.

In the following weeks and months, I struggled to make sense of what was to me senseless. We all did. One night, I went to my dad's new apartment, and I recall the following conversation: "You and Mom took us to church every Sunday, taught our Sunday school classes, and you have always told us that God can do anything. Well, then, why can't he heal your marriage?"

My dad said, "Mac . . . I do think God could heal it. But it would take too long and hurt too much."

I remember thinking to myself, *Take too long and hurt too much for whom!!!? Because this route we're taking right now seems to be taking plenty long and hurting more than enough!*

The Trust Protocol requires of us that we "do what is required." *We have to try.* But the charge to spur someone on to good deeds can never obscure the corresponding charge to love. And that requires attentiveness. We have to tailor our spurring to the person being spurred. There are members of our staff with whom the more direct, pointed, and straight-forward I am, the more they feel valued and honored. With others, I have to be more tactful and more encouraging as I course-correct or critique something they've done that has fallen short of expectations.

I would obviously prefer that Julie approve and celebrate every decision, sermon, leadership move, or parenting choice that I make. The fact is, though, sometimes I blow it. I drop the ball. And when that happens, I need her to tell me. I *want* her to tell me when I've messed up. But *how* she tells me is as important as *that* she tells me. After twenty-six years of wedded bliss, parenting two children into adulthood, planting a church, and more missteps than I care to count, I know that she absolutely has my best interest at heart. She truly wants only God's best for me and for our family.

Paul encourages the Christians in Ephesus to speak life and love and truth to one another with these words:

> We will speak the truth in love, growing in every way more and more like Christ, who is the head of his body, the church. He makes the whole body fit together perfectly. As each part does its own special work, it helps the other parts grow, so that the whole body is healthy and growing and full of love. (Eph. 4:15–16 NLT)

We will speak the truth in love. Yes, we have to try. But we must always try from a posture of love, respect, and honor. Paul concludes that same thought like this:

> Get rid of all bitterness, rage, anger, harsh words, and slander, as well as all types of evil behavior. Instead, be kind to each other, tenderhearted, forgiving one another, just as God through Christ has forgiven you. (Eph. 4:31–32 NLT)

What is it that empowers this kindness, this tenderhearted forgiveness? The answer may surprise you: courage. It takes a courageous heart to love enough to confront in love. By the time we are adolescents, we are all too familiar with the risks associated with loving another person. Parents have disappointed us. Siblings have shrieked at us. Teachers or coaches have come up short in our eyes. Friends have turned on us. We have probably even tasted romantic disappointment. These offenses and wounds conspire to convince us that the risk isn't worth the reward, and that the best move is to play it safe. C. S. Lewis wrote,

> To love at all is to be vulnerable. Love anything, and your heart will certainly be wrung and possibly be broken. If you want to make sure of keeping it intact, you must give your heart to no one, not even to an animal. Wrap it carefully round with hobbies and little luxuries; avoid all entanglements; lock it up safe in the casket or coffin of your selfishness. But in that casket—safe, dark, motionless, airless—it will change. It will not be broken; it will become unbreakable, impenetrable, irredeemable.[3]

You have to try.

7

The Best Teacher You Ever Had

Seeking and Accepting Accountability

Who's the best teacher you ever had? Take a moment and get a clear mental image of that person. Maybe instead of a teacher, it was a coach, a manager at work, or a mentor of some other kind. It might have been someone in middle school, or it may be a mentor you're currently working with. More than likely, they engaged you in a specific class, sport, or industry, but their impact transcended their particular platform and radiated out into other areas of your life that you still draw from today. I want you to lock that person in mentally and put yourself back in that learning environment that was so productive and so crucial to your personal development.

For me, that's an easy question to answer. It was my mom. Throughout her life so far, she has worn a number of different professional hats. She's been a stay-at-home mom, high school guidance counselor, executive assistant, graduate student (twice, both times after she was forty-five years old!), and the volunteer president of a nonprofit museum. But, of all the jobs she's held and the work she's done, at her core, my mom is a teacher.

At seventy-four years old, she still lights up when she describes that moment when a student who has struggled to grasp a subject suddenly gets it. She was teaching high school English when I was born, and she returned to the classroom when I was in the seventh grade. Specifically, she returned to *my* classroom that year as my teacher for English and creative writing. It's a surreal experience to have to figure out how to address your mom when you raise your hand for help in her classroom (*Mom . . . Mrs. Richard . . . Teacher . . . Uhhh, ma'am . . . !!??*).

I remember classmates making jokes about her giving me extra help at home on my papers or answers before a quiz and realize they had absolutely no idea whom they were talking about. She was scrupulously fair, but there was *zero* extra help coming my way.

My mom was a tough grader, especially when it came to papers and reports that had to be turned in. Two or three times, I asked her to look over an assignment before it was due and to give me some help as my mom and not my teacher. It was only two or three times, because that was the year I learned not to ask for feedback unless you *really* want it. With the benefit of thirty-five-plus years of hindsight, I can see that she was absolutely right in her critiques and suggestions, but I wasn't particularly receptive to them then. I wasn't receptive because (a) she's my mom, and (b) I'm stubborn. I'm not proud of that, just keeping it real.

Who's the best teacher/coach/mentor you ever had? Got someone in mind? Obviously, I can't know who is lodged in the frontal lobe of your brain at this moment, but I can tell you something that I know to be absolutely true about that person: he or she was hard on you. Like my mom did as my English teacher, they pushed you. They prodded you to be, do, and accomplish more than you realized you were capable of. They believed in you more than you believed in yourself. More than likely, you got mad at that person at some point or points along the way. But they pushed you, challenged you, and stretched you beyond what you thought you could do.

Here's something else I know because they pushed you: you got better. You grew and developed and expanded your capacity for work, or insight, or compassion for other people, or whatever it was they demanded more of you than you knew you were capable of.

More to the point, you *let* that person push you. At some level, at some time, you decided to let them push you because you discovered that you could trust them. You realized they were pushing you because they believed in you. And because they knew more about the subject or the work than you did, you decided to let them lean in and press you.

Everyone is better—everyone *does* better—when we're coached or challenged. Our greatest growth typically occurs when someone pushes us to reach beyond what we believe we're capable of accomplishing or achieving. Rare is the person who is so intrinsically motivated in every area of life that they don't need coaching or mentoring. And by rare, I mean nonexistent. No one is so self-aware and so objective that they never need help to improve and grow and develop.

Almost as rare is the kind of relationship that allows, or even embraces, that kind of challenging and pushing. That kind of trust-driven accountability and course-correcting is a gift of the highest order. It allows us to reach higher and live stronger, more resilient lives. And the good news is that growth and development in one area almost always bleed over into other facets of life.

Obviously, some teachers or managers far exceed the bounds of pushing and challenging and venture into browbeating and bullying, and that disqualifies them from holding the office of mentor. Far too many people have justified and rationalized abusive behavior by calling their tactics demanding or challenging, or by dismissing those who wouldn't stand for it as weak or fragile.

Similarly, far too many of us have bailed out of challenging situations that could have been highly helpful and beneficial because we didn't like the tactics or the tone of voice employed by the person pushing us. Our temptation, maybe even our *tendency*, in these situations is to focus on the manner of the person rather than the message.

My sophomore year in high school, I had a basketball coach who had a set of pipes that could fill a gymnasium with both sound and fury. Huge voice box. But one day after a particularly tough practice at which he made us run a ridiculous amount of wind sprints and horses,[1] the coach gathered us all at midcourt. Instead of yelling, he spoke in a very calm, rational voice. He said, "Guys, listen. I know I pushed you hard today. I push you hard every day. But never forget this: you've got nothing to worry about as long as I'm yelling at you. The only time you need to worry is if I'm *not* yelling at you."

In an athletic environment, especially among men and young men, yelling and intensity are often a part of the game. Sometimes it's more about distance across a field or gymnasium than it is intensity or anger. The point is not the yelling part of that moment. That was the manner of his delivery.

The message of what he was saying has stuck with me ever since that day. If you care, you push, you challenge, you critique. If you don't care, you let things slide. You ignore or disregard or overlook. When you love someone, as Christians are commanded to do, you do not let things slide; you do not ignore, disregard, or overlook. When we're on the receiving end of that critique or evaluation, spiritual maturity and self-awareness call us to consider the message even when we don't care for the manner in which it's given.

The Bible says, "As iron sharpens iron, so one person sharpens another" (Prov. 27:17). It's a familiar passage that has been printed on a zillion Christian T-shirts and coffee mugs. Yet it's one that we rarely embrace because iron sharpening iron always entails discomfort and struggle, sometimes even outright pain. But it always produces a result greater than the discomfort required to get there and is more than worth it.

When my son, Joseph, was a freshman in high school, he was quarterbacking one of his school's freshman football teams. The morning after their first preseason scrimmage, they gathered in the team's film room to review game film. Since they were freshmen, they had never had the privilege of sitting in a darkened room while the coach reviewed their performance from the night before.

As a quarterback, Joseph got the lion's share of the coach's attention in that Saturday morning film session. When I saw Joseph a couple of hours afterward, I asked him how it went.

Without skipping a beat, he said, "Dad. It sucked." (We do *not* advocate the use of that verb in our home, but sometimes it just is what it is. Talking man-to-man that morning, I decided to let it slide.) I asked him why it had been so bad. "We just went over and over every mistake I made last night. I thought I had played okay until I saw the tape."

I wish I could tell you that I had pondered and prayed for months over what came out of my mouth next, but I replied almost reflexively, "Well, I get it. But if you can learn to take criticism, learn from it and get better, you'll be ahead of about 95 percent of the population." As soon as the words came out of my mouth, I realized that we were talking about much, much more than Texas football in August. Isn't it amazing that God uses something as fleeting as preseason football to teach us eternal truths and principles? (I say that preseason football is fleeting, recognizing of course that *regular* season football is absolutely a matter of life and death.)

When iron sharpens iron, a whole world of subterranean work is fueling the Trust Protocol. First of all, iron sharpening iron involves a certain amount of friction, which creates heat and sparks that can singe or ignite anything flammable nearby. When people enter into a trust-driven relationship or agreement, they agree to be pushed and challenged, to be shown on the game film where they could have done better or made a better decision. The military refers to these kinds of debriefings as After Action Reports (AARs), and they are crucial in identifying mistakes for the purpose of avoiding them in the future.

Sometimes these conversations create sparks that become raging infernos. Some people get fired up and then fire out because they're defensive about their performance, or sparks are generated because the person offering the critique has moved from observations about performance to observations about personality. Either way, fires erupt, and those fires steal necessary oxygen and energy from the relationship or the work; they can take inordinate amounts of time and energy to extinguish.

Second, when iron sharpens iron, the friction also creates abrasions, scuffs and scratches in both pieces of iron. But it's the friction that sharpens the blade so that it reaches its full effectiveness. The scuffs and scratches are only minor, especially in comparison to a blade that is dull and ineffective, and they can be buffed out once the sharpening is complete. But while it's happening, the abrasions are not pretty, and they're not easy to take.

There's another dynamic at work when iron sharpens iron. It's so obvious that most of the time we miss it when we quote this verse or print it on a T-shirt. If iron is being sharpened, it's being done so *for a purpose*. No one takes the time to sharpen something for no reason. We sharpen things for specific purposes.

Last year, our family had the opportunity to visit London. While we were there, I made it a point to visit the shop (shoppe?) of Purdey & Sons Rifle Makers. Since 1814, the Purdeys have been making bespoke shotguns and rifles for hunters and sportsmen and women, from presidents and prime ministers to kings and queens. For a mere £100,000 ($130,000!), they will begin your order, allowing of course for upgrades to satisfy any whim or feature you can dream up.

Not having £100,000 on me at the time, I set my sights instead on a knife made by the Purdey craftsmen. There were multiple options to choose from: folding, hunting, pocket, multitool, trapper, and so on. Finally, I settled on a beautiful skinning knife made of Damascus steel with the Purdey logo notched into the top of the blade. That knife has a specific purpose. It could possibly be used for something *close* to its original intent, but it's best when used for the purpose for which it was designed and crafted. With a three-inch blade, it's never going to be used as a machete to hack through a rain forest or carve through the carcass of a Yukon moose.

When we talk about iron sharpening iron, it is mandatory that we understand what purpose we're pursuing for those being sharpened. What is it that God wants to do in *them* and through *them*? What are his purposes that require sharpened instruments to accomplish and facilitate? It's at this exact juncture that one of the most misunderstood, misapplied, and misleading terms of influence undercuts so many aspiring leaders.

There is a myth afoot within the vast majority of recent writing and speaking that extols the virtues and values of "servant leadership." More often than not this message sacrifices the responsibility of true leadership on the altar of a misguided notion of some kind of communal kumbaya. As if the group, church, or team—or most devastatingly of all, the family!—were some kind of democratic state in which everyone gets a vote on what ought to be done and how it ought to be accomplished.

Servant leadership itself is not a myth. Servant leadership is absolutely the biblical model of leadership and influence that God has ordained, blessed, and endorsed. Clearly, by any rational objective standard, Jesus is the single greatest "leader" or "influencer" the world has ever known. Even someone who doesn't believe that he is the Son of God who rose again on the third day would have to concede that no one else even comes close to having influenced more people. And, to be sure, Jesus did serve those he led and instructed his followers to do the same. He did actually get down on his knees and wash the feet of his closest followers. He said explicitly that he came to serve and not to be served. But in addition to washing feet and equipping and serving his followers, Jesus also sharpened those he served. He was not afraid to create friction and grind some rough edges when necessary. In Matthew 16, the Bible records a remarkably direct iron-sharpening exchange Jesus had with Peter, just a few verses removed from his naming Peter the rock upon which he would build his church. Jesus began to explicitly describe for his disciples the suffering that awaited him in Jerusalem. As was his habit, Peter spoke up: "But Peter took him aside and began to reprimand him for saying such things. 'Heaven forbid, Lord,' he said. 'This will never happen to you!'" (Matt. 16:22 NLT).

That's completely understandable from Peter and the other disciples' perspective. This was their rabbi, their friend, their Lord. Peter's response to Jesus's prediction of suffering makes complete sense.

It's absolutely understandable and dead wrong. Look at how Jesus responds to Peter: "Jesus turned to Peter and said, 'Get away from me, Satan! You are a dangerous trap to me. You are seeing things merely from a human point of view, not from God's'" (Matt. 16:23 NLT). At that moment, Jesus was not washing feet. He was bringing the heat. Jesus perfectly models for us the fact that the two are far from incompatible. This is the same Jesus who drove the money changers out of the temple at the business end of a whip, called the Pharisees a "brood of vipers," and unapologetically owned his role as the Son of God when Pilate asked him if he was a king. Jesus was no milquetoast or shrinking violet. He was and is the very embodiment of the Trust Protocol. His motives and purposes are beyond reproach. He earned the credibility to truly sharpen those he leads. *That* is the model of servant leadership.

The *myth* of servant leadership is this: that we can somehow escape or mitigate our responsibility to lead and hold others accountable under the auspices of "servant" leadership. As followers of Christ, we must not only accept but also embrace our *responsibility* to sharpen, challenge, and speak the truth in love to each other. This is the only way that we are sharpened for the purposes God has called us to both collectively and individually.

And we must embrace our responsibility to sharpen and challenge with *their* best interests in mind. It can be so easy to misappropriate Proverbs 27:17 and correct someone under the camouflage of our own self-interest or insecurities. This is where the *servant* part of leadership—and the love component of the Trust Protocol—come into play.

There's one other thing we must do here as well. We must embrace people who will play that role in *our* lives. We need to have the emotional and spiritual wherewithal to be willing to subject ourselves to truth-telling and iron-sharpening friendships and relationships. It is *our* responsibility to seek out godly counsel and trusting accountability.

Accountability is the act of a true friend or ally. Relational accountability flows out of affinity. Here's why: each and every one of us is accountable in direct proportion to the amount of trust we place in the people holding us to account. If we trust that the people holding us accountable are godly, wise, and shrewd and have our best interest at heart, then we are much more likely to be open, honest, and forthcoming with them. If we don't trust them, then we'll tell them what we think they want to hear and feign transparency in order to check the box that says we're accountable.

In government, publicly traded companies, churches, and nonprofits, there has to be executive oversight that guards against abuses of power, financial improprieties, and other exploitive mischief. Similarly, our individual lives need oversight, especially from the people closest to us. The greatest accountability I have in place in my life is my wife, Julie. We live together, work together, and play together. She knows everything about me: where I go, with whom I meet, my computer passwords, browsing history, spiritual challenges and struggles, insecurities, how much money I spend and where I spend it. There is nothing—I repeat, *nothing*—off-limits to her.

God has blessed me with a few friends of incredible character and amazing depth and breadth of faith. These are the men I have offered an open door to my life; they can ask me anything, anytime, about any part of my life, and I'll shoot them straight. The only thing off-limits to them is the personal side of my marriage, but the health and welfare of it, they're welcome to inquire about. I want that accountability; I crave that accountability in my life.

Every year, Lake Hills Church pays for a third-party audit of all our financial transactions and procedures. Over the years, it has grown to become a rather lengthy process that absorbs a lot of time from Mike Valiton, our Pastor of Finance and Operations, and his team. And it is not an insignificant out-of-pocket expense for us. But the cost of that audit is minuscule compared to the peace of mind that I have knowing our financial ducks are in a row and we're administering well and wisely the resources that God and our people have entrusted to us. That accountability—self-imposed, thorough, and transparent—gives us an absolutely priceless peace of mind.

My mom is a phenomenal teacher. As I recall, she and I both enjoyed the year I was in her class. And we decided that one year was enough. But long before she taught me grammar, literature, and mythology in her classroom, she had always shown me the gift of love and accountability.

In that order.

8

The Chicken or the Egg? Yes

Choosing to Trust before the Evidence Is All In

I was incredibly blessed to have been born into a home where my mom and dad were both believers in Christ; they reared my brothers and me in a comfortable, loving home and were very deliberate about discipline, doing your best, and all the essentials that great parents strive to impart to their kids. Even when my dad left and my parents divorced, I was able to see that my dad had been a really good father through my early childhood and had helped build into me the spiritual and emotional wherewithal that I would need to get through that season of confusion and hurt.

Before I ever realized it or knew what to call it, I had discovered early on that I could trust my parents. They were attentive, engaged, fair but firm disciplinarians—especially by modern standards—and they proved by their actions and provision for us that they were trustworthy.

I realize that not everyone grows up like this. Many people I've known grew up and turned themselves into contributing members of society by sheer force of will. They discovered that to survive and perhaps even dare to thrive, they had to rely on themselves. While they are pleasant enough socially, easy to be around, and good conversationalists, in their heart of hearts many of them simply do not trust. Anyone.

Maybe the most tragic consequence of this acquired distrust is the fact that in every relationship, business transaction, or relational interaction, they are always hedging their bets. Frequently, often without even realizing it, they are planning escape routes, leaving themselves an out—in short, keeping their options open. This begs the question, "Should I trust *before* or *after* I've seen evidence that someone is trustworthy based on their actions?"

Which came first, the chicken or the egg? When this dilemma is applied to our relationships, the Trust Protocol dictates that the answer is really very simple: Which came first, the chicken or the egg? *Yes.*

My wife tells me that I am by nature a very trusting person. Part of my personality makeup is that I shoot pretty straight—at times, to a fault. Not that this is ever a mistake, but I have been known to shoot straight with perhaps a little more gunpowder than was really necessary. I'm a fairly passionate person, and I tend to speak my mind, at times rather directly. Sometimes that's helpful. Sometimes, not so much.

Since Julie is the wisest person I know, we frequently debrief after difficult conversations or meetings that were especially challenging. It's a fairly routine part of our debrief for me to tell Julie what someone in the meeting said or how they responded, and for her to ask me, "Do you think that's true?" My natural bent is to believe people are telling me what they're really thinking. But, as a *pastor*, and as the leader of our staff, I sometimes fail to realize that not everyone feels comfortable shooting straight with me. It's at least possible that sometimes people tell me what they *think* I want to hear rather than what they're actually thinking or feeling.

Julie and I just celebrated twenty-six years of marriage. I trust her. Period. Without even thinking about it, I take the first step in a conversation with her assuming that she's got all her cards on the table. She knows the same about me. If I tell her something that's not true or accurate, it's because I don't have all the information or I misread a situation. We have the comfort and luxury of *assuming* each other is trustworthy, because we have built a résumé of reliability.

But what if you're a recent college graduate starting a new job with a new boss? Or what if you're the manager who just hired the recent college graduate, and you're trying to determine how adaptive, smart, and hardworking your new employee is? At this point, you both have a choice to make: you can hedge your bets, play your cards extremely close to the vest, and wait and see how trustworthy the other person will prove to be. Or you can feed the fire of the trust engine and choose to operate in good faith that the other person is someone worthy of trust.

The risks associated with the latter course of action are obvious. If they're not trustworthy, you get burned, and they have an advantage over you. Or they manipulate, misrepresent, or mistreat you. And it may even cost you financially. None of that is any fun whatsoever. The advantages, however, are greater than the risks, though not as obvious. Let's look at the advantages—the blessings—of choosing to trust before all the evidence is in.

Playing loose. My whole life, I've loved sports. I've always enjoyed competition and being in the game versus watching the game. My junior year of high school, I made the varsity basketball team, but I didn't earn a starting spot. We played several games that year that went down to the final buzzer or even overtime before they were decided. My senior year, I did get to start a few games. I noticed whenever I was in the game, even when it was going down to the wire, I loved playing because I could contribute to the outcome. I was participating versus spectating. Watching a nail-biter from the bench was much more nerve-racking than being on the court.

When we choose to trust someone before we've got a body of work to examine and evaluate, it helps us to play loose and focus on the actual "game" being played, whether it's at work, in a new school, on a team, or in any new environment. When we withhold our trust and hedge our relational bets, we're reacting instead of proactively living in the moment as a contributing member of that relational team. Not only are we withholding our trust, we're withholding our best self, our best effort, and our best work because we're spending some of that energy evaluating and assessing other people's trustworthiness rather than wholeheartedly engaging.

Planting freely. Throughout the Bible we're told that when we give generously of our finances, we will be refreshed and resourced anew. Second Corinthians 9:6 says, "Remember this: Whoever sows sparingly will also reap sparingly, and whoever sows generously will also reap generously." In this verse, Paul is explaining to the church at Corinth the spiritual blessings of material generosity. While this is of course true financially, it's also true in ways beyond money.

When we're generous in our spirit, we reap a generous harvest relationally. When we're generous with our thoughts and perspectives, especially as they relate to other people, our minds and our hearts expand and grow.

Thinking positively. Paul said three things remain: faith, hope, and love. And if you have to pick a winner among the top three, love wins. But look at how love feeds hope. The love of God is the ultimate reality. He *is* love, after all. It's not just something he does or gives; he *is* love. Because he is love, he created us for relationship. And because he loves us, we know that he is for us and with us, and nothing can ever separate us from his love. So no matter what circumstances swirl around us or what situations threaten to swamp us, we *know* that he will sustain, protect, and provide us with *everything* we need. The ultimate expression of that love is, of course, the death, burial, and resurrection of Christ. Our hope is rooted in the rugged reality of the resurrection. Because our hope is based on facts, we can approach every day, every challenge, every obstacle, and every problem with hope, optimism, and a positive perspective.

Living joyfully. When we choose to trust before all the evidence is in, we assume the best about other people. We look forward to our days, our meetings, and our interactions with others. There's an expectation of God's goodness that permeates everything we do and see. I know, I know, it's a dog-eat-dog world out there. I can't just walk around with my head in the clouds pretending that everything's okay and everyone I deal with is going to be a Boy Scout or Girl Scout.

Nowhere does God call us to live head-in-the-cloud—or head-in-the-sand—lives of denial and fantasy. But he does tell us that "the joy of the Lord is my *strength*," "be strong and courageous," "do not fear," "be not afraid," and Jesus said that it's his will that our "joy would be complete."

Playing loose, planting freely, thinking positively, and living joyfully—that is quite an impressive list. It makes for an impressive, God-honoring spiritual résumé if we actually put it into practice. What about when you *do* take the risk and choose to trust before all the evidence is in and that trust isn't reciprocated? Or it isn't returned in the manner you expected? Or the return on your investment of trust costs you more than it benefits you?

Here's the thing: that *will* happen. Guaranteed. If you choose to live generously and trust someone who hasn't yet proven that they can be trusted, at some point that trust will be unappreciated and unreciprocated. When that happens, remember, you're not alone and you're not crazy. Hundreds of thousands of Trust Protocol practitioners just like you have tasted that same disappointment and rejection. You're not alone, but neither are you entitled to integrity from other people.

If you were going to create a playlist of the greatest stories of the Bible, "Jonah and the Whale" would have to be on that list. (I know the Bible says "great fish," but I'm using the title most people are familiar with.) I think an equally fascinating story is "Jonah and the Plant."

Obviously, "Jonah and the Whale" is a classic: Jonah, the prophet of God, responds to God's calling to preach to the pagan citizens of Nineveh by agreeing to go. Then he proceeds to book passage on a ship sailing in the exact opposite direction, only to be discovered by the crew to be the cause of a deadly storm. Thrown overboard, he is swallowed by the great fish and lives in the belly of the beast for three days before being belched up on the shore of, lo and behold, Nineveh! Realizing he's been given a second chance, Jonah follows the Lord's directive and preaches repentance and forgiveness to the Ninevites. Then he retires to the outskirts of the city to await the smell of sulphur and smoke from the imminent judgment of God.

But a funny thing happened on the way to the fire and brimstone. The Ninevites *actually* repented. They abandoned their paganism and their human sacrifices and turned to the God of Israel, who responded in his amazing grace and stayed the judgment that Jonah had told them was coming. Great story, right? Everybody wins, right?

Wellll . . . Jonah didn't see it that way. He complained bitterly to God (spoiler alert: this rarely goes well for the complainer):

> But to Jonah this seemed very wrong, and he became angry. He prayed to the Lord, "Isn't this what I said, Lord, when I was still at home? That is what I tried to forestall by fleeing to Tarshish. I knew that you are a gracious and compassionate God, slow to anger and abounding in love, a God who relents from sending calamity. Now, Lord, take away my life, for it is better for me to die than to live." (Jon. 4:1–3)

Can't you just hear the entitlement dripping off Jonah's attitude and prayer? "Isn't this what I said, Lord?" I'll give him credit for a bold move in taking that kind of attitude with God, but then the entitlement degenerates and deteriorates into melodrama: "It is better for me to die than to live."

Then God shared his grace and goodness with Jonah just as he had with Nineveh. And here is the beauty of the story "Jonah and the Plant": though it doesn't get nearly as much play as the one about the big fish, it is equally significant in what it teaches us about God's character.

> Jonah had gone out and sat down at a place east of the city. There he made himself a shelter, sat in its shade and waited to see what would happen to the city. Then the Lord God provided a leafy plant and made it grow up over Jonah to give shade for his head to ease his discomfort, and Jonah was very happy about the plant. But at dawn the next day God provided a worm, which chewed the plant so that it withered. When the sun rose, God provided a scorching east wind, and the sun blazed on Jonah's head so that he grew faint. He wanted to die, and said, "It would be better for me to die than to live."
>
> But God said to Jonah, "Is it right for you to be angry about the plant?"
>
> "It is," he said. "And I'm so angry I wish I were dead."
>
> But the Lord said, "You have been concerned about this plant, though you did not tend it or make it grow. It sprang up overnight and died overnight. And should I not have concern for the great city of Nineveh, in which there are more than a hundred and twenty thousand people who cannot tell their right hand from their left—and also many animals?" (Jon. 4:5–11)

Did you notice the phrase that is used three different times in those seven verses? *The Lord God provided . . . God provided . . . God provided.* First God provided the leafy plant to protect Jonah from the sun. Next he provided a worm that caused the plant to die. Then he provided a scorching wind to increase Jonah's longing for the shade of the plant. Then he said in so many words, "Jonah, you did *nothing* to deserve the plant in the first place, but you missed it, you longed for it. That's how I miss, how I long for my children to return to me when they abandon me! The city of Nineveh was so blind, so lost in their sin and brokenness, that they didn't know their right hand from their left. Shouldn't I have more concern for them than you do for your silly little plant!?"

I think it's fascinating that with that rhetorical flourish from God, the biblical book of Jonah ends. It's like we're following a trail, looking for clues and answers, and it suddenly stops at a rock wall. We don't learn any more about how Jonah responded, what happened to Nineveh in the wake of their revival, or how, or even if, God continued to work through and with Jonah.

I have a theory why the story of Jonah ends so abruptly. It's not a story about Jonah. It's a story about God and who he is, his holiness, attributes, and compassion. We're entitled to absolutely none of those things. And so again, we're reminded that life is not about us. No matter how badly we want it to be, no matter how consistently we act like it is, no matter how frustrated we get when we discover that it's not, it's not about us. The experience and blessing of those things in our lives are a by-product of God's grace to us.

When we're deciding whether to put ourselves out there, whether to trust *before* or *after* someone has proved himself trust*worthy*, the Trust Protocol requires that we take the lead. That we risk the disappointment, the frustration, and the personal loss and play loosely, plant freely, think positively, and live joyfully. This is our calling, our mission, and our privilege.

Whether we feel like it or not.

9

"How Many Can You Do When You're Tired?"

Choosing Grit over Quit

In the spring of 2010, I was shaking hands after church when a friend from college introduced me to a couple she'd invited to church. Web and Lindsey Smith and their daughter Alexis were relatively new to Austin and looking for a church home, but that's not what I remember most from our introduction.

I knew they were visitors because Web was wearing a sport coat. Guests at Lake Hills Church are never singled out or highlighted. But we know who they are just the same because they either wear their Sunday best or they're on time. For some reason, as Web and I shook hands after that service, with my left hand I clapped him on the shoulder. I remember thinking, *That's weird—how'd he get that cantaloupe under his jacket?* It was obvious as my hand hit solid muscle that this guy was an athlete.

Later that week as we were contacting first-time visitors, I saw that his email address ended with crossfitchron.com. I looked up the website and discovered it was his blog that chronicled his and Lindsey's journey as a couple doing this thing called CrossFit®.

Today, unless you've been living under a rock, you know about CrossFit. But in 2010, burpees, WODs, muscle-ups, thrusters, and the like weren't yet household names of workout elements devised in the bowels of hell.

With some trepidation, I emailed Web and inquired about the possibility of him training me. As you already know, I played the game of basketball in my youth. Over the years and into middle age, while not maintaining the fitness of a triathlon competitor, I had managed to stay relatively un-fat. But I was inviting Web into the weakest part of my life and asking him to help me get stronger, healthier, and better.

Very early in our training, Web introduced me to a physical intensity I'm not sure I even knew in my high school basketball days. It wasn't uncommon for him to devise devilish workouts that lasted only seven, eight, or fifteen minutes but had me on the ground with a heart rate of 180 or more. It was brutal. And I loved it.

One session in particular stands out in my memory, not because of the workout itself but because of something Web said. Marathon runners speak of hitting the wall—that place at mile seventeen or eighteen where your mind decides your body has had enough. In my experience with CrossFit, just about every individual WOD (Workout Of the Day) has a wall of its own.

One of the most common terms in the CrossFit lexicon is *unbroken*, which means that no break is taken between or during individual elements in a workout. As I was progressing through this particular WOD, I wasn't taking a break per se, but let's just say I was taking my time transitioning between the elements. As I got on the floor to do push-ups after racing through some box jumps, I was lying there "transitioning" when Web got on the floor beside me and said, "C'mon, Mac . . . How many can you do when you're tired?"

How many can you do when you're tired? I thought at the time, *How many can YOU do when YOU'RE tired??!!* I probably thought some other less-than-flattering things about him too, but the point is, I have gone back to that moment many, many times since then in situations and circumstances that have nothing to do with physical fitness.

I let Web push me that day—and a lot of other days—when I was facedown or flat on my back in a pool of my own sweat, exhausted, ready to quit, and wanting to give myself a break. But I kept going. Further than I wanted to. Longer than I thought I could. More than I felt I should.

That's the beauty of the Trust Protocol: we not only tolerate but also *embrace* people who push us and challenge us to work harder, dig deeper, and be better at whatever it is we do that really matters. *How many can you do when you're tired?* is a great question for those in a whole host of situations in life that wear us out:

- A wife who's frustrated with her husband
- A father who can't seem to connect with his teenage son

- A pastor who's tired of sermon preparation (*strictly hypothetical*)

- The mom of toddlers who just wants to take a bath or enjoy adult conversation instead of changing one more diaper and cleaning up another spill

- The single woman who lets another man walk out of her life because she's holding out for God's best

- The student who won't compromise his faith and integrity just to be accepted

- The business professional who forgoes a monster bonus because she won't cook the books at the end of the quarter

- The husband who ends a conversation with a coworker who's dissatisfied with her marriage and looking for comfort

How many can you do when you're tired? What that question is getting at, what it's actually asking is, do you have grit? If variety is the spice of life, grit is the protein of life. Grit builds emotional and spiritual muscle to keep going when you feel like quitting, to persevere when you're tired, spent, or angry and can't see a way out or through.

GRIT

The Trust Protocol demands grit. To build trust and to sustain trust over time require that we *choose* grit over quit and keep fighting for the relationship, for the vision, for the good of the whole over the comfort of the self.

I married the most beautifully stubborn woman in the world. That may sound like a paradox, but it's not. Julie, like me, can be stubborn—in the best ways, about the things that matter most. Her personality tends to be easygoing about most things; she doesn't get too worked up about much. *But*—and this is a huge *but*—the things that she does care about, the things that really matter to her, she will dig her heels in and hold on to with a pit-bull determination that is absolutely beautiful and sometimes scary to behold.

Sometimes, just like I do, she digs in and holds her ground in areas that I don't think are a big deal. But, time and again throughout the course of our twenty-six years of marriage, she has chosen to dig in and do the work, have the hard conversations late into the night, work to rediscover the unity we committed to, and lovingly call me out when I'm fooling myself and trying to take her along with me. How many can you do when you're tired? That is grit.

In order to make sure we don't confuse grit with selfish stubbornness, let me give you a working definition that's planted in the fertile soil of Scripture:

God-honoring
Relentless
Intentional
Tenacity

The biblical record of the life of Daniel provides a PhD-level seminar in grit. We first meet Daniel as an adolescent Israelite living in Babylonian captivity some six hundred years before Christ. Though a slave, Daniel stood out from his countrymen and was chosen among a handful of Israelites to apprentice in the palace of Nebuchadnezzar. In this program, Daniel was eligible for treatment and privileges unavailable to the rest of his community. He would have been educated in the protocols of the king's court, elevated above his peers, and relieved of virtually all the burdens common to the typical Israelite slave living in Babylon.

Against this backdrop, God cultivated in Daniel a deep, abiding grit that Daniel would draw from throughout his life. In the palace was where Daniel first chose grit over quit. Having been selected to serve there, he and his friends were to be trained for three years before entering the king's service. One of the perks of this program authorized Daniel and his friends to be fed from the royal table. It doesn't take too much imagination to speculate that their menu would be *significantly* superior to that of the slaves not working in the palace. But look at how Daniel responded:

> Daniel was determined not to defile himself by eating the food and wine given to them by the king. He asked the chief of staff for permission not to eat these unacceptable foods. Now God had given the chief of staff both respect and affection for Daniel. But he responded, "I am afraid of my lord the king, who has ordered that you eat this food and wine. If you become pale and thin compared to the other youths your age, I am afraid the king will have me beheaded." (1:8–10 NLT)

In this brief exchange, there is much for us to discover about how to develop and deploy GRIT in our lives.

God-Honoring

The first characteristic of biblical grit is that it is God-honoring rather than self-serving. The Bible says that Daniel was determined not to *defile himself.* To *defile* something means to taint or stain it in some way. We know that God created us in his image. We are first and foremost unique among all of creation, the image bearers of God himself. That's a big deal.

So our first job in this world, the primary reason we're here, is to represent *accurately* the character and nature of God. When we fail to do that, we're literally distorting the image of God.

When we tell a lie as young kids, or first express the inherent selfishness that is a part of who we are, we are actually defiling ourselves and, by extension, the image of God in us. For Daniel and for us, it's all about honoring, or accurately representing the character and nature of God who stamped us with his image.

Maybe you're a student, and it's just accepted that academic cheating is a part of what you do. If you choose to cheat, you are deciding to defile yourself. You are misrepresenting who God is. To do the right thing when nobody else around you is, *that* requires grit. It requires a conscious decision to determine, "I will be the woman, I will be the man God created me to be, and I will not defile myself by cutting corners, by being dishonest."

Relentless

To live a life of God-honoring grit demands that we make conscious, deliberate decisions to *choose* grit over quit. Over

125

and over and over again. Relentlessly. Daniel's determination not to defile himself was not a one-and-done decision. He and his allies had to continue to choose not to defile themselves. Each step along their path of persistence presented them a fork in the road: one branch of the road was marked QUIT, and the other was marked GRIT.

The first two chapters of Daniel read like the biography of a political prodigy: all career vital signs pointing up and to the right, success after success, promotion after promotion. But chapter three throws the brakes on the Success Express.

Nebuchadnezzar had built a golden idol ninety-feet tall and decreed that all Babylon should bow down and worship it at the sound of the musical blast. Shadrach, Meshach, and Abednego shared Daniel's determination not to defile himself and refused the king's order. King Neb flew into a hysterical rage and summoned them to question their defiance.

> Shadrach, Meshach, and Abednego replied, "O Nebuchadnezzar, we do not need to defend ourselves before you. If we are thrown into the blazing furnace, the God whom we serve is able to save us. He will rescue us from your power, Your Majesty. But even if he doesn't, we want to make it clear to you, Your Majesty, that we will never serve your gods or worship the gold statue you have set up." (Dan. 3:16–18 NLT)

They were *relentless* in their determination. They persisted in their faithfulness. It wasn't a sometimes thing. It was an all-the-time thing.

The most striking aspect of their relentlessness was its unconditional surrender. They had surrendered their will, their actions—their very *lives*—to the will of God. Not even

God's choice to intervene on their behalf, or not, would cause them to waver. To choose grit over quit demands an unwavering commitment to do the right thing and let the chips fall where they may—even if it means walking through the fire.

Intentional

I may not know you, your situation, or your circumstances, but I do know something about you: you will *never* drift into grit. No one will. To live a life of God-honoring grit demands that we make a conscious decision to *choose* grit over quit. It has to be an all-the-time lifestyle and not just a sometimes special event.

Look at how the Bible begins the record of this conversation: "Daniel was determined." Isn't it amazing what we can do when we're determined? Other translations say he "purposed in his heart." We have to determine, we have to set our minds and our hearts on grit. Daniel was *determined* not to defile himself.

Part of being determined requires that we choose our battles wisely but fight to win.

Our daughter, Emily, recently graduated college, but when she was much younger, Emily had a very . . . well, *distinct* taste in clothes. We never talked about it at home, never sat down with her and said, "This is good. This is bad. Make sure that it matches that, and certainly, *never under any circumstances*, wear sequins before six!" In retrospect, perhaps we should have, because she had a serious affinity for sequins.

It was not uncommon for Emily to accompany her mom and brother to Target wearing a sequined unitard with a pink tutu around her waist. I remember initially being somewhat surprised—okay, *dumbfounded*—that Julie, who dresses very conservatively and in day-to-day life prefers comfort over style, had signed off on that wardrobe selection.

Julie decided very early on, when we realized that Emily was a strong personality, that some battles were just not worth fighting. So Julie often walked into Target with Emily in her sequined unitard. Julie would try to walk a little bit ahead of her so that they were distanced from each other, to create some ambiguity as to who this child's parent was, but she was not going to fight that battle.

It's worth noting that the Bible says Daniel *asked* the captain of the guard if they could eat a different diet. He understood authority. Even though the captain of the guard was not God's chosen, and even though Nebuchadnezzar was not by any stretch a God-fearing dictator, Daniel was still under that authority. So he asked if they could eat from a different menu. There is a powerful lesson in this. The Bible says that the chief of staff had respect *and* affection for Daniel. God had given Daniel favor with him—*credibility*. Daniel was not a troublemaker. He did not approach the captain of the guard and say, "I have madeth a commitmenteth. I must not partaketh of the king's foodeth. Taketh it thou away!" He was a normal human being operating within a chain of command, and he simply asked, "Would it be okay if we did something a little bit different?"

I want to encourage you not only to pick your battles and fight to win but also to pray for wisdom when you pick those battles. Ask God. The book of James tells us, "If any of you lacks wisdom, you should ask God, who gives generously to all without finding fault, and it will be given to you" (1:5).

Ask God for wisdom to know which battles are worth fighting. Then stay in the fight, and fight to win.

Tenacity

When Daniel approaches the chief of staff with the request for a different menu, the captain of the guard initially says, "No, it's not okay. If you don't perform, if you don't look as good as the other youths who have been selected for the king's service, I could lose my head." Daniel then does something very important and very shrewd:

> Daniel spoke with the attendant who had been appointed by the chief of staff to look after Daniel, Hananiah, Mishael, and Azariah. "Please test us for ten days on a diet of vegetables and water," Daniel said. "At the end of the ten days, see how we look compared to the other young men who are eating the king's food. Then make your decision in light of what you see." The attendant agreed to Daniel's suggestion and tested them for ten days.
>
> At the end of the ten days, Daniel and his three friends looked healthier and better nourished than the young men who had been eating the food assigned by the king. So after that, the attendant fed them only vegetables instead of the food and wine provided for the others. (1:11–16 NLT)

You know what's interesting to me about people of grit? They perform. They do a good job. They're the ones who get to work on time or a little bit early and are there at the end of the day and maybe a little bit beyond. They're the ones whom the boss knows he can rely on, he can depend on.

129

Nassim Taleb is a world-renowned mathematician, statistician, and author. In his book *Antifragile*, he writes,

> If antifragility is the property of all of those natural (and complex) systems that have survived [the environment, human beings, animals], depriving these systems of volatility, randomness, and stressors will harm them. They will weaken, die, or blow up. . . . Just as spending a month in bed (preferably with an unabridged version of *War and Peace* and access to *The Sopranos'* entire eighty-six episodes) leads to muscle atrophy, complex systems are weakened, even killed, when deprived of stressors. . . . This is the tragedy of modernity: as with neurotically overprotective parents, those trying to help are often hurting us the most.[1]

Of course, there are times when we are fragile. We, especially men, may not like to admit this. But there are times when we are hurt, when we're crushed, when we're broken. That's not what Taleb is referring to. We have been created in the image of God, and it is *in Christ* that we have the opportunity to be more than conquerors. *Nothing* can separate us from the love of God.

Daniel's story of grit continues:

> When the training period ordered by the king was completed, the chief of staff brought all the young men to King Nebuchadnezzar. The king talked with them, and no one impressed him as much as Daniel, Hananiah, Mishael, and Azariah. So they entered the royal service. Whenever the king consulted them in any matter requiring wisdom and balanced judgment, he found them ten times more capable than any of the magicians and enchanters in his entire kingdom. (1:18–20 NLT)

People of grit excel. People of grit do not check the clock and cut corners. People of grit stand out. You know why? Because grit is rare. Our entire nature is geared toward self-preservation and comfort. Grit is not comfortable.

Let's say that you go to the gym today, and it's legs day. You go hard—squats, dead lifts, heavy weights. You're even grunting a little and maybe letting the weights hit the rack a little harder so people notice. I'm just saying. Tomorrow morning, when you first get out of bed, you'll remember today's workout. But it's the second morning after that workout that hits you the hardest. You'll see stars when you get out of bed that morning.

The alarm clock goes off, you *try* to throw your legs over the side of the bed, and nothing moves. The lactic acid has built up overnight and pooled in your muscles. Slowly, you manage to get out of bed, unkink those muscles you'd forgotten about, and start to work out the stiffness and lack of flexibility. You walk to the bathroom to brush your teeth. *Lord, just help me put one foot in front of the other.* You start to go down the stairs and your legs kind of wobble and buckle a little before you grab the railing.

What you've done is stressed those muscles. You've broken them down and taxed them beyond their typical capacity. In the healing process, the miracle, the genius engineering of our bodies, the muscles come back stronger than they were before, and you have to buy all new clothes because all of a sudden you are yoked. The same thing happens through work, through a certain amount of stress. You're better for it. This is how the world that God set in motion works. This is how our lives work best. Grit over quit. You stay after it.

About seven hundred years after Daniel, the apostle Paul wrote to the church in Galatia, explaining to that fledgling congregation how to live out their new faith, how to express what they had experienced. Near the end of his letter to his spiritual children, Paul addresses the issue of grit: "So let's not get tired of doing what is good. At just the right time we will reap a harvest of blessing if we don't give up" (Gal. 6:9 NLT).

Participation in the Trust Protocol is exhausting. Exhilarating, to be sure, but also exhausting. *Let's not get tired of doing what is good.* The promise of God is that when we choose grit over quit, when we endure, when we persevere, we will see the goodness of God, . . . *if* we don't give up.

How many can you do when you're tired?

In Christ, as many as it takes.

10

"Stay on the Bar!"

Building a Community of Trust

Early on a bright January morning three years ago, the temperature in downtown Austin was an unusually cold 23 degrees. I stopped at a tragically hip coffee shop for a little caffeine and warmth before braving the elements to take in the Fittest Games, an annual fitness competition that draws thousands of spectators and hundreds of world-class athletes.

As I pulled up to the site, I was shocked by the hundreds of spectators already milling around before 7:30 a.m. I paid for my ticket and walked through a gauntlet of sponsor tables hawking all kinds of gear and swag for the athletes and athlete wannabes. I walked among hardcore athletes who themselves were only a rung or two below those who would be competing. Even in hoodies and sweatshirts, you could tell they were absolutely yoked.

The first workout of the day was a men's event that would be a series of movements for time:

- Fifty heavy-rope single jumps
- Forty pull-ups
- Thirty thrusters with fifty-pound dumbbells (deep squat, followed by full extension overhead)
- Twenty toes-to-bar
- Ten dumbbell ground-to-overhead with fifty-pound dumbbells

Each of these movements were to be completed *unbroken*, meaning, if the athlete stops or stumbles before completing all the reps, he would have to start over at zero before moving on to the next element.

As the competitors came to the first station, the official gave them a "ready" warning, then began the countdown 3-2-1. At the buzzer, the athletes tore into the first element. Most of them flew through the heavy-rope jumps with no apparent trouble. A couple of them struggled through the pull-ups but completed the element nonetheless. From there it was on to the thrusters, toes-to-bar, and at last the ground-to-overhead lifts. When the first athlete finished the workout, he gathered himself, catching his breath, and waited as others joined him across the finish line.

Finally, there was only one athlete still on the course, and he was stuck on the pull-ups. He would get to twenty-seven, twenty-eight, maybe even thirty, and then fatigue would force him to drop off the bar. But then, a funny thing happened that is typical of that community: rather than watching from the finish line and pitying the athlete still struggling on the course, those who had already finished gathered around him and, along with the spectators, began shouting and encouraging him, "C'mon, man!! You got this! Stay on the bar! Don't let go! Stay . . . on . . . the bar!"

Eventually, he got to the fortieth rep and gritted his way through the final elements of the event before finishing to a thunderous roar from the crowd and backslaps from his fellow competitors.

As I watched that moment unfold, I was as caught up in it as everyone around me. I was yelling and fist-bumping for this guy I didn't even know, urging and encouraging him to *stay on the bar!* And just then, I had the clearest vision of church I'd ever had in my life: *This is what the church is supposed to look like!* Those who are further along in their faith, who've already overcome challenges, hurts, and struggles, circling back to help those who are currently challenged, hurting, and struggling. Encouraging, challenging, and exhorting them: *Stay on the bar! Stay in the game! Don't give up! We're here with you!*

Almost in the same moment, I saw something else instructive for the church: these athletes—from beginners to professionals—make a conscious choice to be pushed and held accountable physically. They show up three, four, or five days a week, and in their workout community, they push each other to grow, develop, and improve. It's not something they do passively once a week or sporadically. Rather than run from accountability or push back, they seek it out, consistently and deliberately subjecting themselves to the momentum and movement of the group.

Between 2005 and 2015, CrossFit recorded a growth curve like few other fitness fads before. To be sure, there are numerous critics of the movement, but the numbers are undeniable. In 2005, there were thirteen CrossFit gyms in the United States.[1] As of 2017, there are more than thirteen thousand around the world.[2] The principles and theories behind the WODs and programming are hardly new or revolutionary. So how do you account for the growth, popularity, and passion of this phenomenon?

In a word, *community*. Few concepts have been as overused, misunderstood, and misappropriated in the last twenty-five years as this one. From the church to cities and towns and internet groups, *community* has come to hold myriad meanings for multitudes of people, based on who is using it and why. Like any other buzzword, its overuse obscures and confuses what is actually meant.

But we still seek it. We still want it. We still need it. There is something in us that yearns to belong, to connect with God and other people. At the same time, though, we seek comfort, ease, and safety. And there's the rub. We cannot connect—genuinely and passionately—in comfort, ease, and safety. To truly connect relationally requires a willingness to dig in and hang on.

A few years ago, I was tarpon fishing with my good friend David Hughes. Our guide, Drew, had anchored up to intercept tarpon as they were swimming along a line just off the beach. After we'd been in this one spot for five to ten minutes, we noticed that the wind and waves had us drifting off the line where we wanted to be. Drew pulled up the anchor and motored back to where we wanted to be, threw the anchor out, and we started looking for fish again.

About five minutes later, we noticed we were again drifting when we heard our guide taking off his shirt and flip-flops. Things can quickly get weird in the Keys, but he stopped his disrobing there and dove into the water off the poling platform on the back of his boat. We watched him swim the length of the boat, follow the anchor chain down to where it was in about six to eight feet of water, and drive it into the ocean floor. He swam back to the surface and climbed back on board, and we started fishing again.

Here's what I learned that day: the anchor only holds if you dig in. Our relationships are only as durable as our willingness to dig in and hold on, no matter how hard the winds blow or how high the waves go.

Have you ever heard someone say, "God won't give you more than you can handle"? We want to believe that's true, and that platitude may provide some temporary comfort. But it will be temporary, because the fact is that God will absolutely allow challenges, struggles, hurts, and wounds into our lives that we can't handle. They will require that we dig in more deeply, more personally, and more penetratingly to him, his power, and his grace.

When we read and learn about faith, our relationship with Christ, and how faith changes and grows in response to challenge, we are more likely to persevere. Through perseverance, we grow, develop, and mature.

Hebrews 10–12 is actually a graduate and postgraduate study in exactly that: what faith is and how it changes and grows in response to challenge. But it's not just an academic study. It is a call to live life on a higher plane, empowered by the Holy Spirit to abandon the status quo and what passes for normal. It's a radical restructuring of our priorities, what we prize and what we pursue.

Because here's what I believe:

- I believe that deep, deep down we want to be men and women who are tough enough to choose to love and lead their homes—spiritually and financially—and who refuse to passively let life happen to them, their spouses, and their kids.
- I believe that we want to be parents who are more concerned about teaching their kids the ways of God than improving their speed and ball-handling skills.
- I believe that deep, deep down we want to be tough enough to tackle the tasks of everyday life without the help of a bottle to take the edge off and acting like fugitives escaping from the reality we've created for ourselves.
- I believe that we can raise kids tough enough to not drink their way through high school and college and who will choose to guard the gift of their sexuality for marriage.
- I believe that deep, deep down we want to be tough enough not just to invite someone to church but also to stand up for our faith and our beliefs, no matter the cost.

And I believe that exactly none of that happens over time without Jesus.

The author of Hebrews helps us to focus our faith on the things that matter—both now and eternally. This is put-on-your-grown-up-pants-and-let's-go faith. As you might have guessed, Hebrews was originally a letter written to a group of, well, *Hebrews*, who were wrestling with how to live out this new faith in Christ, in light of the fact that they had grown up in and around the Jewish faith and culture.

We don't know who the author of Hebrews is; there are parts that sound a lot like Paul's letters and other parts that don't sound anything like Paul. What we do know is that the book of Hebrews was included in the canon—the books of the Bible supernaturally communicated and supernaturally translated from God to people for his purposes. Hebrews 10:19–25 makes a reference to the old Jewish system of sacrifices that sustained their covenant with God before Christ. Look at what the author says in verse 23: "Let us hold unswervingly to the hope we profess, for he who promised is faithful."

This is really the kicker for this chapter. I love that word *unswervingly*. Let me give you a good definition of *unswervingly*: no matter what. Hold on to the hope we profess—that God so loves us that whoever believes in him will never die but will have eternal life, beginning right here, right now. Hold on to that hope and profess that hope unswervingly—*no matter what*.

Remember the day I was fishing with David Hughes and our guide stuck the anchor? There's a part of the story I didn't tell you: about thirty to forty-five seconds after Drew climbed back into the boat, we spotted a shadow in the water swimming toward us. David got ready to cast, but Drew said, "Wait—that's not a tarpon." And before he could say more, we saw a six-foot bull shark coming straight toward us. He had apparently picked up on his radar Drew's splashing and thrashing in the water when he was sticking the anchor.

Here's another lesson I learned that day: when you're swimming in shark-infested waters, you better have a boat.

The church is our boat in shark-infested waters. The writer of Hebrews is telling us that the church—the family of faith—is an anchor for our faith. We are not only better together, we are also tougher together, safer together—but only to the degree that we dig in. Psalm 92 tells us that we flourish when we are *planted* in the house of God (vv. 12–13).

Too often, we treat church as an obligation or an opportunity to score religious points for attending, when in reality we *need* the church. *I've never seen anyone, any family, move away from the church and get better.* The church is the body of Christ, the soil in which we put down roots of commitment and relationship—*community*, in the most powerful, beautiful, and God-honoring sense of the word. That community challenges us, sharpens us, and refines us to be everything God created us to be. It's where we are used for his purposes and his glory. It's the family who circles around us when we feel like giving up, when we feel like we can't go on, and who reminds us in love and good deeds to stay on the bar!

11

But I Live in the Real World

Benefiting the Bottom Line

Some of the most fun I've ever had in my life was coaching my kids' sports teams before they graduated to *actual* coaching at the middle-school level. I've always been pretty competitive despite my own limited athleticism, but I always wanted to help every kid on those teams have as much fun as possible.

During one game in Joseph's elementary years of baseball, I was yelling from the dugout trying to get the attention of one of his teammates who was wandering aimlessly around the outfield, blissfully oblivious to the game going on around him. I wasn't angry with him; I just didn't want him to get beaned in the head with a baseball on my watch. After the game, Julie told me that while I was trying to get this young man's attention, she heard a dad in the bleachers say to his friend about the coach yelling in the dugout, "*That* guy is a *pastor*!!??"

I've noticed in over thirty years of ministry that people respond in some really fascinating ways to the fact that I'm a pastor. I remember a time in college when a girl asked me what I was thinking about doing after graduation. She was noticeably taken aback when I told her I was called into ministry. She stammered in response, "Oh, that's . . . that's really . . . nice." Sometimes when I see people in a restaurant, they'll try to nonchalantly drape their napkin over the bottle of beer accompanying their enchiladas, apparently so as not to offend the pastor's sensitive morals.

Maybe even while you've been reading this book about trust, love, and good deeds, you've thought, *Yeah, well, easy for you to say—you're a pastor. Everybody you work with is a Christian. Where I work, it's not that easy. You can't just walk around "loving people" all the time. I have to produce. I have to hit my numbers and justify my place on the team, or I lose my place on the team, or If I focused exclusively on meeting my husband's needs (demands?), mine would never even be considered.*

I acknowledge the differences between our day-to-day environments and the motives of the people who inhabit those environments. But while there may be some built-in advantages for implementing the Trust Protocol where I work, you actually may have a greater opportunity for it than I do.

Allow me to submit something for your consideration: What if . . . *what if* . . . your day-to-day world, which appears to be an impediment to the Trust Protocol ever taking root and bearing fruit, is actually an *advantage* that you could leverage for God's glory and your good? If you traffic in that kind of a space, the Trust Protocol can be the most potent weapon at your disposal.

Let's say for the sake of conversation that your workplace really is just too "real-world" for the Trust Protocol to ever take root. Okay, fine. Then it follows that the people you work with are guarded, skeptical, closed off, driven by self-interest, and out for number one—not necessarily because they're bad people but because they've seen that's the kind of behavior that gets rewarded, especially financially.

If that's the case, how much *more* would someone stand out who volunteers to clean the break-room kitchen without being asked *and* meets quota every month? How much *more* would someone in that culture stand out who offers to help their secretary or assistant close out the quarterly reports because it's a tedious job, while also managing a high-performing division? How much *more* would a manager stand out who gives an employee a personal day to attend to their mother who is in assisted living and growing more disoriented, while also consistently producing company-leading results?

What might appear as a weakness can actually—*over time*—be leveraged as a strength. It's spiritual and relational jujitsu. Many practitioners of Brazilian jujitsu compare it more closely to chess than warfare. It's more about reading and responding to your opponent than simply charging in and subduing them. Central to this physical chess match is the principle of *leverage*. With leverage, smaller fighters can find a way to turn an opponent's apparent advantage in strength and power into a weakness that works against them.

Given that the Trust Protocol works, and that it restores, renews, and reinvigorates every environment and interaction that it touches, those environments where it isn't the prevalent paradigm are at a decided disadvantage. The relational jujitsu martial artist wisely uses this disadvantage to their advantage and *leverages* it to highlight the strengths and benefits of building trust in that space.

Jesus actually anticipated our real-world objections to the kind of life that he calls us to live. The Bible records one of the first probing missions of the Trust Protocol. Jesus sends the disciples out on a short-term mission project. He tells them to team up with a partner, leave their money and bags behind, and focus exclusively on the people of Israel. This was essentially a training exercise for his followers because Jesus would be there waiting for them when they returned. There would come a time when he wouldn't be physically present after sending them out, but that was for a later date. Here's what he told them:

> I am sending you out like sheep among wolves. Therefore be as shrewd as snakes and as innocent as doves. Be on your guard; you will be handed over to the local councils and be flogged in the synagogues. On my account you will be brought before governors and kings as witnesses to them and to the Gentiles. But when they arrest you, do not worry about what to say or how to say it. At that time you will be given what to say, for it will not be you speaking, but the Spirit of your Father speaking through you. (Matt. 10:16–20)

Sometimes, we mistakenly think that the real worldliness of this world is news to God, as if he somehow just doesn't get how harsh and depraved and cold this world can be. But it was exactly his understanding of the brokenness of this world that drove him to abandon heaven and inhabit earth for the forgiveness of our sins and the restoration of his order and sovereignty. It was the brokenness of this world that nailed him to a cross when he had never committed a sin, much less a crime.

Therefore be as shrewd as snakes and as innocent as doves. Be shrewd, be wise, be discerning. Jesus commands us to be wise precisely because he knows all too well just how broken and dog-eat-dog this world really is. He promises us we will suffer. We'll be arrested, turned over for questioning, abused, betrayed, punished, ridiculed, and mocked.

It's really a misguided, presumptuous arrogance to think that we have an insight into how the world operates that is superior to the One who created the world in the first place. But Jesus doesn't leave it there. He tells us not to worry about what we'll say or how we'll say it. The Spirit of God will speak through us!

Repeat after me: It's not about me. *It's not about me.* Playing our part in the Trust Protocol transcends our comfort, our wisdom, and our plans. Playing our part in the Trust Protocol is about our trusting—*innocent as doves*—that God is God, that he is all-knowing, all-seeing, all-present, all-powerful, and obeying and collaborating with him—*shrewd as snakes*—in his redemptive work.

Robert and Kelly (not their real names) had been married less than six years. They had met, fallen in love, and begun a whirlwind courtship with lots of fun, adventurous travel, nightlife, and almost constant partying. Unbeknownst to Kelly when they met, Robert had a long track record of womanizing, using sexual conquest to measure his masculinity and sense of self-worth. Though he genuinely cared for

Kelly, old habits are tough to break, and his unfaithfulness to her began soon after they started dating and continued after their wedding.

For her part, Kelly had suspicions that she choked down and chose to ignore. From time to time, she'd discover a stray phone number or some other sign of Robert's wandering attention, but she never confronted him because she didn't want to face the reality that he might be doing exactly what she suspected.

Then, something quietly but unmistakably broke in Robert. He sat down and confessed everything to Kelly. In an attempt to rebuild their marriage, he confessed to multiple liaisons, explaining that he felt as if something was broken in him and he needed her to help him figure it out and fix it. Understandably, Kelly was devastated by his confession and left their house in tears.

How's that for *real world*?

A few hours later, after driving around Austin processing Robert's revelation, she gathered herself and walked back in the house where he was waiting. She told him that she thought she could forgive him, but she didn't know how to fix their marriage. Recalling their story years later, she said, "I can't explain it, but when he told me everything that day—all the times he'd betrayed me and our marriage—as painful as it was, I'd never trusted him more than I did at that moment. It was as if I knew that if he was telling me all *that*, then there was literally *nothing* between us. It wasn't like that made everything okay, but I knew right then that I could trust this man going forward."

That wasn't the end of the pain and struggle for Robert and Kelly. In fact, in some ways it was just the beginning.

They committed to a path of counseling, prayer, reconciliation, and the restoration of their marriage that continues to this day. What happened that day was relational and spiritual jujitsu: the fragile shell of their marriage, compromised and damaged by Robert's deceit and Kelly's denial, was leveraged for the strength of renewal and genuine intimacy between them.

We need to be careful and make sure that we don't buy the lie that confession or coming clean is going to magically erase all the hurt and brokenness of betrayal. What it *will* do, though, is create a launching pad from which trust can be relaunched, *if*—and this is a major *if*—all parties concerned are willing to wade into the work of rebuilding and reconnecting the trust terminals of love *and* good deeds.

You might say, "But I need this job, I have to put food on the table" or "If I want to play football [or swim, or dance, or play in the band] at the next level, I have to satisfy my coaches where I am." These objections are real and valid. But never forget: you *always* have a choice. You are not a victim. You decide where you invest your skills and heart and soul in work. If you don't like the environment, change it or leave it.

This is one of the great advantages of the Trust Protocol: precisely because you are developing your love *and* good deeds, your good deeds—your capacity for work, your skills, the value you add to a team—make you a person with options. If all you are is a nice guy or a nice girl, then you will have to tolerate and stomach horrible bosses, conniving coworkers, and untrustworthy clients. But as you develop your skills and increase your capacity to produce great work, your value and worth to a team grow and your options multiply exponentially. You become someone whom quality organizations want to have, someone they will make room for because of the value you bring.

But you don't know how I've been betrayed . . . You don't know where I work . . . You don't understand the family that I come from . . . My coaches are not *interested in trust, only about winning at all costs.* Toxic environments are real. I get that. I've seen them, and I know how soul-starving they can be.

But the reality is that no team or organization will ever out-trust its leadership. If the leadership of an organization cultivates or tolerates a duplicitous, every-man-or-woman-for-themselves environment, then that is the ethos that will prevail. This is an immutable, universal law of organizations and teams: the point person determines the trust quotient of the team. That person will set the pace and establish the ceiling of trust for the team they lead. If you're not the one responsible for the overall culture and health of the team and that culture is toxic, get out.

But I need the paycheck. Really? Let me get this straight: the God who parted the Red Sea for Israel and raised Christ from the dead is somehow unable to provide for you and your family as you seek to honor him and follow him in integrity *and* action? The One who feeds the birds of the air and clothes the fields of the earth, the One who knows when a single sparrow falls to the ground is going to be spread too thin to meet your material needs as you serve and glorify him in faith?

Just because you may not see a path to survival and paying your bills without the paycheck you currently count on does *not* mean that there isn't a path that God has already carved out for you. He is waiting for you to take that first step of faith before he lights the next step for you.

It's a hard world. Jesus knows that. He knows that better than we know it. But he also knows something that we sometimes forget. When we say we live in the *real world*, we mean to say that it's not always easy to do the right thing. The fact of the matter is, this real world is actually a poor, poor facsimile of what God originally intended this world to be. But in his truly amazing grace and awesome power and strength, he is very deliberately and intentionally working this world—and us—toward a new creation that restores, renews, and redeems everything that was lost to sin.

That is the *real* real world we're longing for.

12

Staying Power

Cultivating Strength through Trust

I t was the best of times, it was the worst of times." Charles
Dickens was describing revolutionary Paris in the opening of his classic *A Tale of Two Cities*. He just as easily
could have been describing the pain and joy that Julie and I
experienced when we dropped both of our kids off at college.
It's a rite of passage that you pray for, prepare for, work for,
and save for, but it is one of the most difficult things we ever
do as parents.

We thoroughly enjoyed every stage of their growing-up
years. Like every family, we had our ups and downs, challenges and setbacks, arguments and disagreements. But Emily
and Joseph both made the teen years some of the best we
ever had as a family. When they left home to start college,
as excited as we were for them and the opportunities they

would encounter, we knew that a significant part of our lives was changing and would never be the same again.

Both of our kids went away to school, South Carolina to be specific—Emily to the College of Charleston and Joseph to Clemson University. We knew when we dropped them off that we wouldn't be seeing them on weekends. Leaving Emily in her dorm room and Joseph at his truck are two moments seared in my memory that were absolutely the best of times and the worst of times.

When we left Emily, Julie and I were flying back to Austin, so we had a set deadline for leaving in order to make our flight. We had been scurrying around Charleston making trips to Target and Home Depot for supplies and tools to get her all moved in. As the time for our departure approached, we all knew it was coming and started to avoid making eye contact.

Finally, we could avoid it no longer and had to say our good-byes. We hugged, cried, hugged some more, and finally left her to figure out her new life on her own—which she did in the most amazing ways. It was a bright, hot August day in the Deep South; Julie and I walked out of Emily's dorm room and went straight to the airport. We sat side by side on the plane still wearing our sunglasses and fighting back tears throughout the entire flight. I would regain my composure only to lose it again moments later. Julie would squeeze my hand, and I'd get myself together, only to realize that it was now her turn. We traded serve on the emotions all the way back to Texas and for a few days after we got home.

It was the best of times, it was the worst of times. Leaving Emily at college that day and Joseph two years later were the worst days of my parenting career. I hated it. Not because they weren't ready or because I feared they would go off the deep end in college. But we had enjoyed the teen years so much, and I knew that season of life was gone and wouldn't return. As right as it was that they graduated high school, and as much as we celebrated the fact that they were ready to move on to the next phase of their lives, Julie and I grieved that milestone. We were going to miss having them around the house, music blaring from behind their bedroom doors, sharing movie night, laughing together.

In the middle of that hurt, I discovered one of the sweetest, richest blessings I've ever tasted. In the middle of letting our kids go, I found that in sharing it all with Julie—in letting my guard down and telling her that I missed Emily sitting on the foot of our bed at 11:15 at night and the sound of Joseph singing at the top of his lungs in his room—there was something deep, powerful, and profound. All of a sudden, we discovered a whole new vein of love and commitment we weren't looking for or even knew was possible. Holding hands on the plane back to Texas, we were both grieving, but we got to do it *together*.

What we discovered was *staying power*.

Staying power is perhaps the most beautiful and most powerful payoff of the Trust Protocol. It's not the power *to* stay. It's the power that comes *from* staying. It's the power that is cultivated and developed when we choose to stay—in a marriage, a job, a church, a friendship—and is only realized and experienced *after* the staying has occurred.

The trust that is nurtured and cultivated in the best of times and the worst of times is a natural consequence of the character and nature of God. In Romans 5, God shows us how this trust and peace and struggle all work together for his glory and our good:

> Therefore, since we have been justified through faith, we have peace with God through our Lord Jesus Christ, through whom we have gained access by faith into this grace in which we now stand. And we boast in the hope of the glory of God. Not only so, but we also glory in our sufferings, because we know that suffering produces perseverance; perseverance, character; and character, hope. And hope does not put us to shame, because God's love has been poured out into our hearts through the Holy Spirit, who has been given to us. (vv. 1–5)

To be justified by faith means that we are declared right with God in Christ. The grace of God makes us aware of our need for forgiveness, for reconciliation with God, since our sin made us enemies of God.

But look what else justification does for us: *because* Christ makes us right with God, even our suffering is redeemed in Christ. *We glory in our sufferings* doesn't mean that we adopt a masochistic enjoyment of the suffering itself or that we blithely deny the reality of suffering. It means that in Christ, we are given a new, eternal perspective that allows us to see the power and sovereignty of God as he redeems our suffering. As only he can do, he cultivates within us perseverance (power *for staying*), and through that perseverance our character is shaped and molded to be more like his. In the development of our character, we discover the power of hope to persevere, to persist, and to prevail.

Having had the blessing and the privilege of pastoring the same church for twenty-plus years, I've had the opportunity to baptize the children of parents whose weddings I performed. I've gotten to be there with families who've lost loved ones at every stage of life, from the very young to the very old. Though the families were grieving and I grieved with them, there's an undeniable blessing and privilege in walking through those seasons with them. Through the seasons, the trust and credibility we share grow and deepen, and the power of our connection intensifies.

Staying power.

And I almost missed it.

In the early, formative years of Lake Hills Church, there were two times when I didn't think we were going to make it. Honestly, there were more than two times, but these two really stand out among the others. In one of them, we didn't know if we would survive financially. The needle on our finances read *below* the big E on the dial. In the other, I didn't know if *I* would make it. I was tired and worn down from the preaching, visiting, vision-casting, and everything that was required to get this beast off the ground and into the air.

In both of those dire instances, I stopped and looked at the situation at hand. *Right* at hand. I didn't see how we would last another month. But I knew we had enough fuel—financially, emotionally, and spiritually—to have one more weekend worship service. We could take one more step and see if God might open a door and give us enough oxygen to live to fight another day.

And he did. In neither of those instances did we receive a windfall contribution that extended our financial runway another six months. But in both of those instances and dozens more like them, God's grace was sufficient for us to take one more step in faith and see where he led after that.

Perseverance may be the most critical life skill we parents ever teach our kids. I know beyond a shadow of a doubt that Emily and Joseph are going to encounter challenges and struggles, heartbreak and loss along the way. Jesus promised us that in this world we will have troubles. And I know that I won't be there each time to point the way or light the path and tell them what to do. But Julie and I can—and it's our God-given responsibility to—equip and prepare them to know *that* they can persevere and persist because of Christ and in the power of the Holy Spirit.

One of the greatest disservices we do for our kids is to shield and protect them from failure or struggle. We cripple their faith and their resiliency when we swoop in and rescue them from the natural consequences of their own choices and mistakes.

Years ago, I interviewed Brad and Colt McCoy for a Father's Day sermon. Colt had just completed his career as quarterback for the University of Texas, and his dad had been his high school coach before he attended UT. At one point in our conversation, Brad said, "You know, Mac, we always felt like it was our job as parents to prepare our kids for the path and *not* the path for our kids." When he made that statement, it resonated so deeply and powerfully in me that I interrupted him.

"Wait a minute!" I said. "Say that again!" He repeated the line, and I told him that I was going to steal that line. It's too good. It's too true. Our job as parents is absolutely to prepare our kids for the path and *not* the path for our kids! We can't prepare every path they'll take, every work situation, every friendship or dating relationship, or their own marriage one day. So we need to prepare and equip them for those times when they'll fail, when they'll struggle along the way while they're under the protective covering of our parenting and household.

When they call from the school panicked because they didn't get your signature on something that *has* to be signed today, don't go to the school to sign it. When they tell you at 9:30 at night that they need poster board for a project that's due tomorrow morning, don't rush out to the grocery store in your flip-flops hoping they stock the right size and color. They may get a bad grade; they might even fail a test. But they'll discover some very valuable tools: responsibility and resiliency.

They'll discover that their responsibilities are *their* responsibilities—not yours, not mine. I've already done eighth grade, and I killed it. I don't need to do it again. The other thing they'll learn is what they're capable of coming back from. They'll learn to rebound, to take a shot and get back up and go to work.

We don't always know the reasons why God allows certain things in our lives, but we do know this: when we get to the end of ourselves, we discover the endlessness of God's power. Romans 5 explains how he does this: suffering produces perseverance, perseverance produces character, and character produces hope. I love these words from verse 5, "Hope does not put us to shame." Hope that is rooted in the rugged reality of the resurrection never puts us to shame. Our hope is anchored in the fact of the empty tomb. This isn't some pie-in-the-sky panacea or crutch, as some like to call it. This is a hope based on the fact of a personal experience with the personal God who loves us enough to create us and then redeem us and forgive us all our sins through his only Son Jesus. *That* hope is never put to shame.

By now, you know that Julie and I have been married twenty-six years. But what you may not know is that we almost didn't make it eight years. Like most couples, early on we wrestled with how to figure out each other and marriage. We were head over heels in love, but we had to navigate everything from bathroom courtesies to conflict resolution to whose family to spend holidays with.

One night after we had moved to Austin, we found ourselves on very different pages as husband and wife. We weren't angry with each other, but there was a definite frustration factor on both our parts in the air that night. In a moment of extreme courage and intense uncertainty, Julie said to me, "I think you may have married the wrong person."

It was a moment that scared us both. But in that moment we both dug in and committed ourselves to resolving our frustrations. I chose to lean in and affirm her as my bride; I had *never* quit loving her, choosing her, and wanting her. She leaned in and affirmed me as the husband she still wanted; she never wanted to quit being my bride and building a marriage and a home that we both wanted. We just hadn't gotten very good at communicating those things.

We talked deep into the night—and on more than a few others—and worked and prayed our way into a marriage that not only survived but also flourished and thrived. As we held hands flying home and crying over Emily's departure, it was that specific night when we were much younger and had talked through our doubts and frustrations that I thought about. Because of the *grace* of God and our choosing to tap into it, we could draw on the *power* of God to hold each other up, to encourage, comfort, and love each other when we were hurting.

Since that experience, my confidence in Julie and our marriage has grown and multiplied exponentially. Because of the twenty-six years we have together as husband and wife and the track record she has amassed, her credibility with me is virtually unassailable. I know she's human and fallible, but my trust in her is so complete that I don't even think about it anymore. Trusting Julie is like breathing; it just happens. It's an involuntary muscle that she has exercised and grown over the years of our marriage.

The power of the Trust Protocol—credibility forged through integrity and action—grows through struggle. Rather than being stifled or stymied in challenging situations and environments, relationships grow deeper and get stronger when they're tested and survive to thrive.

Every time.

13

No Exceptions

Why the Trust Protocol Works—Every Time

You might not immediately think of the US Military Academy as fertile soil for things like love and community. It is a place of significant historical importance, incredibly high standards, and rigorous academic and physical requirements. And it's difficult not to be impressed, if not outright intimidated, by the grandeur of West Point. Named for people such as Grant, Lee, Pershing, Patton, Eisenhower, and many others who have secured and defended our nation, the buildings themselves radiate strength and power.

Several years ago, I had the opportunity to meet General Robert Caslen while on a tour of West Point. At the time, he was serving as the commandant of the corps, responsible for every cadet's military and physical development.

General Caslen graduated from West Point in 1975, went on to a distinguished military career that has seen battlefield experience in Afghanistan and Iraq, and has contributed to peacekeeping missions in Haiti.

Walking into the office of the commandant of the corps, you see people who are clearly on task and know what needs to be done and why. Some of the people supporting the commandant are career military themselves who have risen to the rank of colonel. Everyone is cordial and even warm, but this is clearly a place where incredibly skilled and competent people make things happen.

General Caslen is an example of quiet, reserved, raw intensity. In his office he speaks almost softly, but he is clearly fueled by a passion for what he does and the forces he serves. I was anxious to test the validity of the Trust Protocol against the experiences and convictions of this man, who had consciously chosen to devote his professional career to serving his country when he could have opted for a more lucrative career in any number of fields.

As I laid it out to him and shared the concepts of community and accountability, his eyes bored holes through me. When I finished, he took a deep breath and looked out the window for just a brief moment. Then he said,

> I've never put it in those terms before, but it makes sense. Let me show you how we think about this.
>
> This spring, we'll graduate 870 First Years. Within a few months, most of them will be commanding troops in either Iraq or Afghanistan. When they assume command, their troops really won't care that they graduated from West Point. Some will probably even resent it. They'll only be asking

two questions of those new officers: *Are you competent?* and *Do you care?*

If they're competent, then those troops have a better chance of coming home alive. But, if they're competent *and* they demonstrate that they genuinely care about a wife back home who's pregnant or their parents who are managing health problems while they're half a world away, then those troops will really—I mean, *really*—follow them.

For us, leadership really matters because *lives are at stake.*

No matter where you are right now, you have a choice to make. If you're in the mailroom dreaming about the corner office, if you're a part-time, no-pay intern at a multinational corporation or the CEO of a corporation, if you're a stay-at-home soccer mom, if you pastor a world-changing megachurch or you just launched a church plant of thirty-seven people, if you're a classroom teacher to a roomful of six-year-olds—you have the opportunity to make a difference in someone's life, today, right now.

Lives are at stake.

The lives of the people around you, those in your God-given sphere of influence, are waiting to see how you receive, respect, and respond to the mandate that is the Trust Protocol. Most people you come in contact with will never know that this is your mandate, your calling from God. But they will absolutely know whether they can trust you, whether you're a man or woman of your word, and whether your walk matches your talk. It's been said that most people won't remember what we say, but they'll never forget how we make them feel. And how we make them feel—especially those closest to us with whom we live, work, play, pray, and do life—will be based primarily on the degree to which our words correspond to our actions. This is the credibility we forge in integrity and action.

And here's the kicker: there are no exceptions. The Trust Protocol works—every single time.

Every single time we choose to embrace, adopt, and apply the Trust Protocol, we forge that God-honoring credibility in integrity and action that creates confidence, kindles hope, and reduces relational uncertainty and insecurity.

You may be thinking to yourself, *Every single time, huh? Yeah, right. You don't know my boss/husband/child/dad/ wife/employees/friends/coworkers (choose one)!* And you're right, I don't. But I do know this: even in situations where the people around us may not collaborate and participate in the Trust Protocol, even when we are the only ones practicing the Protocol, it helps *everywhere* it's applied. It will improve a hostile work environment, mitigate a dysfunctional family system, upgrade a team's chemistry, and cover over a multitude of credibility sins.

The reason why it makes a difference is because the Trust Protocol reflects the character and nature of God, and God is good. The closest we can get to the biblical concept of God's goodness is the great Hebrew word *shalom*. We think of shalom as Israel's version of Aloha! or Ciao!, a one-word greeting or salutation that covers all our etiquette bases when we're greeting a friend. And it does do that in the vernacular use. But the Hebrew concept of shalom runs much, much deeper than that.

For the Israelites, shalom was the fulfillment of God's promise to provide peace and rest to his chosen people. But it was peace in its fullest sense, not just the absence of war and conflict. The *Dictionary of Biblical Languages* lists the following facets of shalom:

- Peace, prosperity—an intact state of favorable circumstance (1 Sam. 1:17)
- Completeness—the state of a totality of a collection (Jer. 13:19)
- Safeness, salvation—a state of being free from danger (Gen. 28:21)
- Health—a state of lack of disease and a wholeness or well-being (Ps. 38:4)
- Satisfaction, contentment—the state of having one's basic needs or more being met and so being content (Exod. 18:23)[1]

That's some list, isn't it? And it's everything that God promises to those who follow Christ. Certainly, the ultimate fulfillment of these things won't be realized until we are with Christ in eternity, but they are all included in his redemption and restoration that we get to be a part of in this lifetime. These outcomes, these divinely ordered results, are the end game of the Trust Protocol. When we spur one another on toward love *and* good deeds, we are contributing—adding our voices and our blood, sweat, and tears—to the expansion and blessings of the kingdom of God.

These facets of shalom are like the facets of a diamond: they work together to focus and refract the light of God's character in all its brilliance and clarity. And his shalom is more fully realized and revealed in and through the Trust Protocol.

One of the most revealing descriptions of Jesus is given in the Gospel of John as he is introducing us to the central character of the story he's about to convey. In the very first verse, John refers to Jesus as the Word, the *logos*: "In the beginning was the Word, and the Word was with God, and the Word was God" (John 1:1). He proceeds with more preliminary comments, introduces Jesus's cousin John the Baptist, and then makes the following statement: "The Word became flesh and made his dwelling among us. We have seen his glory, the glory of the one and only Son, who came from the Father, *full of grace and truth*" (John 1:14, emphasis added).

Grace and truth are the shalom of God. That grace, that undeserved favor of God, overwhelms us when we experience it, when we taste it and recognize the goodness of it in our lives. It drives us into the arms of a loving Father who loves us too much to lie to us and tell us that our sin doesn't matter or that it's no big deal. The truth is that it *does* matter and it *is* a big deal because it drives us away from him, away from his shalom—his completeness and peace and life and love—not only in this life but also for all eternity. Further, our sin costs us. We pay the price of the natural consequences of our sin in ruptured relationship not only with God but also with each other and with ourselves.

Relationship is the coin of the realm. Whatever we do in life, relationship and connectedness lie at the heart of everything that truly matters. Sin damages our relational capacity and robs us of the gifts and blessings that accompany healthy, thriving relationships. This fact reveals a beautiful part of God's heart for us: part of the reason God takes sin so seriously is because he knows—better than we do—the damage that it does to us and our relationships at home, in the marketplace, among Christ followers, between people of faith and agnostics, on teams, in politics, and in every other relational arena.

When we understand that God hates sin because it opposes his holiness and damages our hearts, we start to see him as the good Father he is rather than as a cosmic referee who's looking for opportunities to blow the whistle on us.

The fact that Jesus came from the Father, full of both grace *and* truth, was manifest most clearly in one groundbreaking, eternity-shaking encounter during his earthly ministry. The Pharisees, those self-appointed religious watchdogs of that era, interrupted Jesus while he was teaching in the temple and threw at him a woman who had been caught in adultery. "'Teacher,' they said to Jesus, 'this woman was caught in the act of adultery. The law of Moses says to stone her. What do you say?'" (John 8:4–5 NLT). Their goal, of course, was to trap Jesus in a theological snare: If he refutes the law of Moses, then they have him dead to rights as a heretic. But if he upholds the law of Moses—the truth—then he contradicts his own promise of forgiveness—the grace.

What a moment. Even two thousand years removed from that scene, you can sense the tension. Jesus, surrounded by a crowd who had come to hear him teach in the temple that morning, confronted with the dilemma of grace *or* truth, had to respond from his heart, from his core. The choice he was given was an either-or, grace or truth. Typical of Jesus, and so powerfully instructive for us, he chose a third way: grace *and* truth. The Bible says he stooped down and began drawing on the ground. When the scribes and Pharisees continued pressing him for an answer, he stood up and said, "'All right, but let the one who has never sinned throw the first stone!' Then he stooped down again and wrote in the dust" (John 8:7b–8 NLT).

I think an alternative paraphrase for verse 8 would read, "Then he dropped the mic." *Boom.* One by one, from the oldest to the youngest, the pack of watchdogs, realizing they were out of their depth spiritually and doctrinally, dropped their stones and walked away. If you or I were directing the movie version of this event, we'd probably fade to black as the last stone fell and the youngest accuser departed. But Jesus wasn't done yet because he wasn't most concerned with making his point. Look at how Scripture concludes this vignette:

> Then Jesus stood up again and said to the woman, "Where are your accusers? Didn't even one of them condemn you?"
>
> "No, Lord," she said.
>
> And Jesus said, "Neither do I. Go and sin no more." (John 8:10–11 NLT)

"Neither do I [condemn]. Go and sin no more." Grace *and* truth. Jesus was more concerned about making a person than making a point. Making the woman whole, complete, restored, valued. Loved.

He communicated that love by speaking to her as a whole person. He doesn't condemn, but neither will he condone. We've created a false dichotomy that to accept us is to accept or tolerate our sin as well. But the gospel tells us that our sin defaces and disfigures the image of God we are created to bear. *I love you too much to lie to you.* Grace *and* truth.

The reality of Jesus's grace-and-truth character, his nature, is the reason why the Trust Protocol works everywhere. When

168

we apply the Trust Protocol, our love and good deeds manifest his grace and truth. He has embedded his personality in creation, in our hearts, in our deepest needs and desires. So whenever we participate in his kingdom work, whenever we emulate his kingdom heart, he is glorified, and he blesses that situation or relationship or circumstance with his presence and power. Because he is all good, all the time, that goodness—that shalom—rubs off on everything it touches.

Our world is literally dying for that kind of goodness. You get to be the pipeline, the conduit and vehicle for the goodness of God to touch everything you touch. This grassroots conspiracy to forge credibility through integrity and action is the most exciting adventure you'll ever know. There will be twists and turns, hills and valleys, bumps and bruises along the way. But it is the life that is *truly* life. It is the only way to fly. It is our calling, our honor, and our privilege.

It is our mandate.

Forge ahead.

Notes

Introduction

1. 2017 Edelman Trust Barometer: Global Annual Study, http://www
.edelman.com/trust2017/.

2. John Adams, argument in defense of the British soldiers in the
Boston Massacre trials, December 4, 1770, The Federalist Papers Project,
http://thefederalistpapers.org/founders/john-adams.

Chapter 1 "I Love You, and I Will Fire You"

1. Steve Schmidt and Bob Shrum, "Falling Trust and Growing Disrup-
tion in the 2016 Election," Edelman, March 11, 2016, http://www.edelman
.com/post/falling-trust-growing-disruption-2016-election/.

Chapter 3 The Revolution Will Not Be Sanitized

1. *Online Etymology Dictionary*, s.v. "integer," http://www.etymon
line.com/index.php?term=integer.

2. Gil Scott-Heron, "The Revolution Will Not Be Televised," recorded
April 19, 1971, on *Pieces of a Man*, Flying Dutchman, RCA Studios,
New York, 33⅓ rpm.

Chapter 5 It's the Relationship, Stupid

1. .38 Special, performance of "Hold On Loosely," by Don Barnes, Jeff
Carlisi, and Jim Peterik, recorded September 1979–July 1980 on *Wild-
Eyed Southern Boys*, A&M Records, Studio One, Doraville, GA, vinyl.

Chapter 6 You Have to Try!

1. Winston Churchill, quoted in Jerry R. Wilson, *151 Quick Ideas to Inspire Your Staff* (Franklin Lakes, NJ: Career Press, 2005), 167.
2. Vince Lombardi Jr., quoted in Jerry Glover, *Play to Win: Keys to Victory in the Game of Life* (Bloomington, IN: iUniverse, 2008), 55.
3. C. S. Lewis, *The Four Loves* (New York: Harcourt, Brace, 1991), 121.

Chapter 7 The Best Teacher You Ever Had

1. Horses (aka *suicides*) is a conditioning drill loathed by generations of basketball players since time immemorial.

Chapter 9 "How Many Can You Do When You're Tired?"

1. Nassim Nicholas Taleb, *Antifragile: Things That Gain from Disorder* (New York: Random House, 2014), 5.

Chapter 10 "Stay on the Bar!"

1. Paul Teetor, "The Story of How CrossFit Went from Zero to 10,000 Locations," *LA Weekly*, August 14, 2014, http://www.laweekly.com/arts/the-story-of-how-crossfit-went-from-zero-to-10-000-locations-5005604.
2. "About Affiliation," CrossFit, 2017, accessed May 16, 2017, https://affiliate.crossfit.com.

Chapter 13 No Exceptions

1. James Swanson, *Dictionary of Biblical Languages with Semantic Domains: Hebrew (Old Testament)* (Bellingham, WA: Logos Research Systems, 1997), Logos Bible Software ebook, s.v. "shalom."

Mac Richard is the founding pastor of Lake Hills Church in Austin, Texas. He and his wife, Julie, launched Lake Hills with a calling to redefine church for the city of Austin and beyond. In 2008, Mac found Spur Leadership to equip and empower marketplace professionals with practical tools to expand their leadership capacity and their contribution to the world.

Mac and Julie have two college-age kids, love any time they get to see them, and are thoroughly enjoying the empty-nest years.